MznLnx

Missing Links Exam Preps

Exam Prep for

Essentials of Contemporary Management

Jones & George, 2nd Edition

The MznLnx Exam Prep is your link from the texbook and lecture to your exams.
The MznLnx Exam Preps are unauthorized and comprehensive reviews of your textbooks.

MznLnx

Rico
Publications

Exam Prep for Essentials of Contemporary Management
2nd Edition
Jones & George

Publisher: Raymond Houge
Assistant Editor: Michael Rouger
Text and Cover Designer: Lisa Buckner
Marketing Manager: Sara Swagger
Project Manager, Editorial Production: Jerry Emerson
Art Director: Vernon Lowerui
Product Manager: Dave Mason
Editorial Assitant: Rachel Guzmanji
Pedagogy: Debra Long
Cover Image: Jim Reed/Getty Images
Text and Cover Printer: City Printing, Inc.
Compositor: Media Mix, Inc.

For more information about our products, contact us at:
Dave.Mason@RicoPublications.com

For permission to use material from this text or product, submit a request online to:
Dave.Mason@RicoPublications.com

Printed in the United States
ISBN:

Contents

TO THE STUDENT

COMPREHENSIVE

The *MznLnx* Exam Prep series is designed to help you pass your exams. Editors at MznLnx review your textbooks and then prepare these practice exams to help you master the textbook material. Unlike study guides, workbooks, and practice tests provided by the texbook publisher and textbook authors, *MznLnx* gives you ***all*** of the material in each chapter in exam form, not just samples, so you can be sure to nail your exam.

MECHANICAL

The MznLnx Exam Prep series creates exams that will help you learn the subject matter as well as test you on your understanding. Each question is designed to help you master the concept. Just working through the exams, you gain an understanding of the subject--its a simple mechanical process that produces success.

INTEGRATED STUDY GUIDE AND REVIEW

MznLnx is not just a set of exams designed to test you, its also a comprehensive review of the subject content. Each exam question is also a review of the concept, making sure that you will get the answer correct without having to go to other sources of material. You learn as you go! Its the easiest way to pass an exam.

HUMOR

Studying can be tedious and dry. MznLnx's instructional design includes moderate humor within the exam questions on occassion, to break the tedium and revitalize the brain

1. _________ is a process of planning and controlling the performance or execution of any type of activity, such as:

- a project (project _________) or
- a process (process _________, sometimes referred to as the process performance measurement and management system.)

Organization's senior management is responsible for carrying out its _________.

a. Human Relations Movement
b. Management process
c. Work design
d. Participatory management

2. _________ is a forward looking process for setting goals and regularly checking progress toward achieving those goals. It is a continual feedback process whereby the actual outputs are measured and compared with the desired goals. Any discrepancy or gap is then fed back into changing the inputs of the process, so as to achieve the desired goals or outputs.
a. 28-hour day
b. Performance management
c. 33 Strategies of War
d. 1990 Clean Air Act

3. _________ is an increasingly broadening term with which an organization, or other human system describes the combination of traditionally administrative personnel functions with acquisition and application of skills, knowledge and experience, Employee Relations and resource planning at various levels. The field draws upon concepts developed in Industrial/Organizational Psychology and System Theory. _________ has at least two related interpretations depending on context. The original usage derives from political economy and economics, where it was traditionally called labor, one of four factors of production although this perspective is changing as a function of new and ongoing research into more strategic approaches at national levels. This first usage is used more in terms of '_________ development', and can go beyond just organizations to the level of nations . The more traditional usage within corporations and businesses refers to the individuals within a firm or agency, and to the portion of the organization that deals with hiring, firing, training, and other personnel issues, typically referred to as `_________ management'.
a. Human resources
b. Bradford Factor
c. Human resource management
d. Progressive discipline

4. _________ comprises the actual output or results of an organization as measured against its intended outputs (or goals and objectives.)

Specialists in many fields are concerned with _________ including strategic planners, operations, finance, legal, and organizational development.

In recent years, many organizations have attempted to manage _________ using the balanced scorecard methodology where performance is tracked and measured in multiple dimensions such as:

- financial performance (e.g. shareholder return)
- customer service
- social responsibility (e.g. corporate citizenship, community outreach)
- employee stewardship

.

a. A4e
b. A Stake in the Outcome
c. Organizational performance
d. AAAI

5. An _________ is a mostly hierarchical concept of subordination of entities that collaborate and contribute to serve one common aim.

Organizations are a variant of clustered entities. The structure of an organization is usually set up in many a styles, dependent on their objectives and ambience.

a. Informal organization
b. Organizational development
c. Open shop
d. Organizational structure

6. _________ is one of the managerial functions like planning, organizing, staffing and directing. It is an important function because it helps to check the errors and to take the corrective action so that deviation from standards are minimized and stated goals of the organization are achieved in desired manner.According to modern concepts, _________ is a foreseeing action whereas earlier concept of _________ was used only when errors were detected. _________ in management means setting standards, measuring actual performance and taking corrective action.
a. Turnover
b. Decision tree pruning
c. Schedule of reinforcement
d. Control

7. A _________ is a list of the general tasks and responsibilities of a position. Typically, it also includes to whom the position reports, specifications such as the qualifications needed by the person in the job, salary range for the position, etc. A _________ is usually developed by conducting a job analysis, which includes examining the tasks and sequences of tasks necessary to perform the job.

a. Job description
b. Recruitment
c. Recruitment advertising
d. Recruitment Process Insourcing

8. _________ has become one of the most popular theories in organizational psychology.

Goal setting has been a formula used for acheivement since the early 1800s. The form and pattern has cahanged drastically over the years and there is still much debate as to what is the most efective pattern to follow.

a. Goal-setting theory
b. Human relations
c. Job satisfaction
d. Corporate Culture

9. In economics, business, retail, and accounting, a _________ is the value of money that has been used up to produce something, and hence is not available for use anymore. In economics, a _________ is an alternative that is given up as a result of a decision. In business, the _________ may be one of acquisition, in which case the amount of money expended to acquire it is counted as _________.

a. Cost overrun
b. Cost
c. Fixed costs
d. Cost allocation

10. In a military context, the _________ is the line of authority and responsibility along which orders are passed within a military unit and between different units. The term is also used in a civilian management context describing comparable hierarchical structures of authority.

a. 1990 Clean Air Act
b. French leave
c. 28-hour day
d. Chain of command

11. A chief executive officer (_________) or chief executive is one of the highest-ranking corporate officer (executive) or administrator in charge of total management. An individual selected as President and _________ of a corporation, company, organization, or agency, reports to the board of directors. In internal communication and press releases, many companies capitalize the term and those of other high positions, even when they are not proper nouns.

a. Chief executive officer
b. Director of communications
c. Portfolio manager
d. CEO

12. A _________ or chief executive is one of the highest-ranking corporate officer (executive) or administrator in charge of total management. An individual selected as President and _________ of a corporation, company, organization, or agency, reports to the board of directors. In internal communication and press releases, many companies capitalize the term and those of other high positions, even when they are not proper nouns.

a. Purchasing manager
b. Chief brand officer
c. Financial analyst
d. Chief executive officer

13. A _________ or chief operations officer is a corporate officer responsible for managing the day-to-day activities of the corporation and for operations management (OM.) The _________ is one of the highest-ranking members of an organization's senior management, monitoring the daily operations of the company and reporting to the board of directors and the top executive officer, usually the chief executive officer (CEO.) The _________ is usually an executive or senior officer.

a. Value based pricing
b. Supervisory board
c. Chief operating officer
d. Product innovation

14. While _________ literally refers to a person responsible for the performance of duties involved in running an organization, the exact meaning of the role is variable, depending on the organization.

While there is no clear line between executive or principal and inferior officers, principal officers are high-level officials in the executive branch of U.S. government such as department heads of independent agencies. In Humphrey's Executor v. United States, 295 U.S. 602 (1935), the Court distinguished between _________s and quasi-legislative or quasi-judicial officers by stating that the former serve at the pleasure of the President and may be removed at his discretion.

a. Easement
b. Unreported employment
c. Australian Fair Pay and Conditions Standard
d. Executive officer

15. _________ is the corporate management term for the act of reorganizing the legal, ownership, operational, or other structures of a company for the purpose of making it more profitable, or better organized for its present needs. Alternate reasons for _________ include a change of ownership or ownership structure, demerger repositioning debt _________ and financial _________.

a. Net worth
b. Market value added
c. Market value
d. Restructuring

16. _________ is subcontracting a process, such as product design or manufacturing, to a third-party company. The decision to outsource is often made in the interest of lowering cost or making better use of time and energy costs, redirecting or conserving energy directed at the competencies of a particular business, or to make more efficient use of land, labor, capital, (information) technology and resources. _________ became part of the business lexicon during the 1980s.

a. Operant conditioning
b. Opinion leadership
c. Unemployment insurance
d. Outsourcing

17. _________ refers to increasing the spiritual, political, social or economic strength of individuals and communities. It often involves the empowered developing confidence in their own capacities.

The term Human _________ covers a vast landscape of meanings, interpretations, definitions and disciplines ranging from psychology and philosophy to the highly commercialized Self-Help industry and Motivational sciences.

a. AAAI
b. A4e
c. A Stake in the Outcome
d. Empowerment

18. _________ refers to various methodologies for analyzing the requirements of a job.

The general purpose of _________ is to document the requirements of a job and the work performed. Job and task analysis is performed as a basis for later improvements, including: definition of a job domain; describing a job; developing performance appraisals, selection systems, promotion criteria, training needs assessment, and compensation plans.

a. Work design
b. Hersey-Blanchard situational theory
c. Management process
d. Job analysis

19. _________ is, in very basic words, a position a firm occupies against its competitors.

According to Michael Porter, the three methods for creating a sustainable _________ are through:

1. Cost leadership

2. Differentiation

3. Focus (economics)

a. 28-hour day
b. 1990 Clean Air Act
c. Theory Z
d. Competitive advantage

20. _________ consists of the processes a company uses to track and organize its contacts with its current and prospective customers. _________ software is used to support these processes; information about customers and customer interactions can be entered, stored and accessed by employees in different company departments. Typical _________ goals are to improve services provided to customers, and to use customer contact information for targeted marketing.

a. Green marketing
b. Disruptive technology
c. Marketing plan
d. Customer relationship management

21. _________ is a form of communication that typically attempts to persuade potential customers to purchase or to consume more of a particular brand of product or service. 'While now central to the contemporary global economy and the reproduction of global production networks, it is only quite recently that _________ has been more than a marginal influence on patterns of sales and production. The formation of modern _________ was intimately bound up with the emergence of new forms of monopoly capitalism around the end of the 19th and beginning of the 20th century as one element in corporate strategies to create, organize and where possible control markets, especially for mass produced consumer goods.

a. A4e
b. AAAI
c. A Stake in the Outcome
d. Advertising

22. An _________ is a person who has possession of an enterprise and assumes significant accountability for the inherent risks and the outcome. It is an ambitious leader who combines land, labor, and capital to create and market new goods or services. The term is a loanword from French and was first defined by the Irish economist Richard Cantillon.

a. A4e
b. AAAI
c. A Stake in the Outcome
d. Entrepreneur

23. In politics, a _________, (by metaphor with the carved _________ at the prow of a sailing ship), is a person who holds an important title or office yet executes little actual power, most commonly limited by convention rather than law. Common _________s include constitutional monarchs, such as: Queen Elizabeth II, the Emperor of Japan, or presidents in parliamentary democracies, such as the President of Israel.

While the authority of a _________ is in practice generally symbolic, public opinion, respect for the office or the office holder and access to high levels of government can give them significant influence on events.

a. Figurehead
b. 1990 Clean Air Act
c. 33 Strategies of War
d. 28-hour day

24. In queueing theory, _________ is the proportion of the system's resources which is used by the traffic which arrives at it. It should be strictly less than one for the system to function well. It is usually represented by the symbol ρ.

a. A4e
b. A Stake in the Outcome
c. Utilization
d. AAAI

25. _________ refers to training in different ways to improve overall performance. It takes advantage of the particular effectiveness of each training method, while at the same time attempting to neglect the shortcomings of that method by combining it with other methods that address its weaknesses.

Cross training is employee-employer field means, training employees to do one another's work.

a. 28-hour day
b. Cross-training
c. 33 Strategies of War
d. 1990 Clean Air Act

26. _________ is a business management strategy aimed at embedding awareness of quality in all organizational processes. _________ has been widely used in manufacturing, education, hospitals, call centers, government, and service industries, as well as NASA space and science programs.

As defined by the International Organization for Standardization (ISO):

> '_________ is a management approach for an organization, centered on quality, based on the participation of all its members and aiming at long-term success through customer satisfaction, and benefits to all members of the organization and to society.' ISO 8402:1994

One major aim is to reduce variation from every process so that greater consistency of effort is obtained. (Royse, D., Thyer, B., Padgett D., ' Logan T., 2006)

a. 28-hour day
b. Quality management
c. Total quality management
d. 1990 Clean Air Act

27. The 'business case for _________', theorizes that in a global marketplace, a company that employs a diverse workforce (both men and women, people of many generations, people from ethnically and racially diverse backgrounds etc.) is better able to understand the demographics of the marketplace it serves and is thus better equipped to thrive in that marketplace than a company that has a more limited range of employee demographics.

An additional corollary suggests that a company that supports the _________ of its workforce can also improve employee satisfaction, productivity and retention.

a. Kanban
b. Trademark
c. Virtual team
d. Diversity

28. The _________ is the labour pool in employment. It is generally used to describe those working for a single company or industry, but can also apply to a geographic region like a city, country, state, etc. The term generally excludes the employers or management, and implies those involved in manual labour.
a. Division of labour
b. Pink-collar worker
c. Workforce
d. Work-life balance

29. _________, commonly known as e-commerce, consists of the buying and selling of products or services over electronic systems such as the Internet and other computer networks. The amount of trade conducted electronically has grown extraordinarily with widespread Internet usage. The use of commerce is conducted in this way, spurring and drawing on innovations in electronic funds transfer, supply chain management, Internet marketing, online transaction processing, electronic data interchange (EDI), inventory management systems, and automated data collection systems.
a. A Stake in the Outcome
b. A4e
c. Online shopping
d. Electronic Commerce

30. _________ is a business magazine published by McGraw-Hill. It was first published in 1929 (as The Business Week) under the direction of Malcolm Muir, who was serving as president of the McGraw-Hill Publishing company at the time. Its primary competitors in the national business magazine category are Fortune and Forbes, which are published bi-weekly.
a. BusinessWeek
b. Democracy in America
c. The Wealth of Nations
d. Hotel Vikas

31. _________ can be regarded as an outcome of mental processes (cognitive process) leading to the selection of a course of action among several alternatives. Every _________ process produces a final choice. The output can be an action or an opinion of choice.

a. 28-hour day
b. Decision making
c. 33 Strategies of War
d. 1990 Clean Air Act

32. _________ has been described as the 'process of social influence in which one person can enlist the aid and support of others in the accomplishment of a common task' . A definition more inclusive of followers comes from Alan Keith of Genentech who said '_________ is ultimately about creating a way for people to contribute to making something extraordinary happen.'

_________ is one of the most salient aspects of the organizational context. However, defining _________ has been challenging.

a. 1990 Clean Air Act
b. 28-hour day
c. Situational leadership
d. Leadership

33. _________ is a theory of management that analyzes and synthesizes workflows, with the objective of improving labour productivity. The core ideas of the theory were developed by Frederick Winslow Taylor in the 1880s and 1890s, and were first published in his monographs, Shop Management and The Principles of _________ Taylor believed that decisions based upon tradition and rules of thumb should be replaced by precise procedures developed after careful study of an individual at work.

a. Capacity planning
b. Value engineering
c. Master production schedule
d. Scientific management

34. The _________ is a form of reactivity whereby subjects improve an aspect of their behavior being experimentally measured simply in response to the fact that they are being studied, not in response to any particular experimental manipulation.

The term was coined in 1955 by Henry A. Landsberger when analyzing older experiments from 1924-1932 at the Hawthorne Works (outside Chicago.) Hawthorne Works had commissioned a study to see if its workers would become more productive in higher or lower levels of light.

a. 28-hour day
b. 1990 Clean Air Act
c. 33 Strategies of War
d. Hawthorne effect

35. _________ Movement refers to those researchers of organizational development who study the behavior of people in groups, in particular workplace groups. It originated in the 1920s' Hawthorne studies, which examined the effects of social relations, motivation and employee satisfaction on factory productivity. The movement viewed workers in terms of their psychology and fit with companies, rather than as interchangeable parts.
a. Work design
b. Participatory management
c. Hersey-Blanchard situational theory
d. Human relations

36. _________ refers to those researchers of organizational development who study the behavior of people in groups, in particular workplace groups. It originated in the 1920s' Hawthorne studies, which examined the effects of social relations, motivation and employee satisfaction on factory productivity. The movement viewed workers in terms of their psychology and fit with companies, rather than as interchangeable parts.
a. Human relations movement
b. Job satisfaction
c. Path-goal theory
d. Job analysis

37. The _________ is the interlocking social structure that governs how people work together in practice. It is the aggregate of behaviors, interactions, norms, personal and professional connections through which work gets done and relationships are built among people who share a common organizational affiliation or cluster of affiliations. It consists of a dynamic set of personal relationships, social networks, communities of common interest, and emotional sources of motivation. The _________ evolves organically and spontaneously in response to changes in the work environment, the flux of people through its porous boundaries, and the complex social dynamics of its members.
a. Open shop
b. Union shop
c. Organizational effectiveness
d. Informal organization

38. _________ and Theory Y are theories of human motivation created and developed by Douglas McGregor at the MIT Sloan School of Management in the 1960s that have been used in human resource management, organizational behavior, organizational communication and organizational development. They describe two very different attitudes toward workforce motivation. McGregor felt that companies followed either one or the other approach.

In _________, which many managers practice, management assumes employees are inherently lazy and will avoid work if they can. They inherently dislike work. Because of this, workers need to be closely supervised and comprehensive systems of controls developed.

a. Management team
b. Theory X
c. Cash cow
d. Job enrichment

39. Theory X and _________ are theories of human motivation created and developed by Douglas McGregor at the MIT Sloan School of Management in the 1960s that have been used in human resource management, organizational behavior, organizational communication and organizational development. They describe two very different attitudes toward workforce motivation. McGregor felt that companies followed either one or the other approach.

In _________, management assumes employees may be ambitious and self-motivated and exercise self-control. It is believed that employees enjoy their mental and physical work duties.

a. Theory Y
b. Contingency theory
c. Business Workflow Analysis
d. Design leadership

1. In psychology, _________ is a major approach to the study of human personality. Trait theorists are primarily interested in the measurement of traits, which can be defined as habitual patterns of behavior, thought, and emotion. According to this perspective, traits are relatively stable over time, differ among individuals (e.g. some people are outgoing whereas others are shy), and influence behavior.

a. Psychological statistics
b. Cognitive dissonance
c. Psychometrics
d. Trait theory

2. _________ is one of five major domains of personality discovered by psychologists. Openness involves active imagination, aesthetic sensitivity, attentiveness to inner feelings, preference for variety, and intellectual curiosity. A great deal of psychometric research has demonstrated that these qualities are statistically correlated.

a. Introversion
b. Extraversion
c. Introverts
d. Openness to experience

3. Negative Affect is a general dimension of subjective distress and unpleasurable engagement that subsumes a variety of aversive mood states, including anger, contempt, disgust, guilt, fear, and nervousness. Individuals high in _________ are characterized by distress, un-pleasurable engagement, and nervousness. Low negative affect is characterised by a state of calmness and serenity.

a. 33 Strategies of War
b. 28-hour day
c. 1990 Clean Air Act
d. Negative affectivity

4. _________ is a term in psychology which refers to a person's belief about what causes the good or bad results in his or her life, either in general or in a specific area such as health or academics. Understanding of the concept was developed by Julian B. Rotter in 1954, and has since become an important aspect of personality studies.

_________ refers to the extent to which individuals believe that they can control events that affect them.

a. Social loafing
b. Locus of control
c. Self-enhancement
d. Machiavellianism

5. _________ is one of the managerial functions like planning, organizing, staffing and directing. It is an important function because it helps to check the errors and to take the corrective action so that deviation from standards are minimized and stated goals of the organization are achieved in desired manner.According to modern concepts, _________ is a foreseeing action whereas earlier concept of _________ was used only when errors were detected. _________ in management means setting standards, measuring actual performance and taking corrective action.

a. Schedule of reinforcement
b. Control
c. Decision tree pruning
d. Turnover

6. _________ is an idea in the field of Organizational studies and management which describes the psychology, attitudes, experiences, beliefs and Values (personal and cultural values) of an organization. It has been defined as 'the specific collection of values and norms that are shared by people and groups in an organization and that control the way they interact with each other and with stakeholders outside the organization.'

This definition continues to explain organizational values also known as 'beliefs and ideas about what kinds of goals members of an organization should pursue and ideas about the appropriate kinds or standards of behavior organizational members should use to achieve these goals. From organizational values develop organizational norms, guidelines or expectations that prescribe appropriate kinds of behavior by employees in particular situations and control the behavior of organizational members towards one another.'

_________ is not the same as corporate culture.

a. Organizational development
b. Union shop
c. Organizational effectiveness
d. Organizational culture

7. A _________ is a person who alleges misconduct. More complex definitions may be used, but the issue is that the _________ usually faces reprisal. The misconduct may be classified in many ways; for example, a violation of a law, rule, regulation and/or a direct threat to public interest, such as fraud, health/safety violations, and corruption.

a. 1990 Clean Air Act
b. 33 Strategies of War
c. 28-hour day
d. Whistleblower

8. In law, _________ is the term to describe a partnership between two or more parties.

In England a number of statutes on the subject have been passed, the chief being the Bastardy Act of 1845, and the Bastardy Laws Amendment Acts of 1872 and 1873. The mother of a bastard may summon the putative father to petty sessions within twelve months of the birth (or at any later time if he is proved to have contributed to the child's support within twelve months after the birth), and the justices, as after hearing evidence on both sides, may, if the mother's evidence be corroborated in some material particular, adjudge the man to be the putative father of the child, and order him to pay a sum not exceeding five shillings a week for its maintenance, together with a sum for expenses incidental to the birth, or the funeral expenses, if it has died before the date of order, and the costs of the proceedings.

a. Affiliation
b. Abraham Harold Maslow
c. Affirmative action
d. Adam Smith

9. In psychology, _________ reflects a person's overall evaluation or appraisal of his or her own worth.

_________ encompasses beliefs (for example, 'I am competent/incompetent') and emotions (for example, triumph/despair, pride/shame.) Behavior may reflect _________

a. 1990 Clean Air Act
b. 28-hour day
c. 33 Strategies of War
d. Self-esteem

10. _________ refers to an individual's desire for significant accomplishment, mastering of skills, control, or high standards. The term was introduced by the psychologist, David McClelland.

_________ is related to the difficulty of tasks people choose to undertake.

a. Two-factor theory
b. Need for power
c. 1990 Clean Air Act
d. Need for achievement

11. _________ is the value of objects, both physical objects and abstract objects, not as ends-in-themselves but a means of achieving something else. It is often contrasted with items of intrinsic value.

It is studied in the field of value theory.

a. A4e
b. AAAI
c. A Stake in the Outcome
d. Instrumental value

12. The 'business case for _________', theorizes that in a global marketplace, a company that employs a diverse workforce (both men and women, people of many generations, people from ethnically and racially diverse backgrounds etc.) is better able to understand the demographics of the marketplace it serves and is thus better equipped to thrive in that marketplace than a company that has a more limited range of employee demographics.

An additional corollary suggests that a company that supports the _________ of its workforce can also improve employee satisfaction, productivity and retention.

a. Virtual team
b. Trademark
c. Kanban
d. Diversity

13. _________ is an attempt to motivate employees by giving them the opportunity to use the range of their abilities. It is an idea that was developed by the American psychologist Frederick Herzberg in the 1950s. It can be contrasted to job enlargement which simply increases the number of tasks without changing the challenge.
a. Job enrichment
b. Cash cow
c. C-A-K-E
d. Catfish effect

14. _________ can be regarded as an outcome of mental processes (cognitive process) leading to the selection of a course of action among several alternatives. Every _________ process produces a final choice. The output can be an action or an opinion of choice.
a. 28-hour day
b. 33 Strategies of War
c. 1990 Clean Air Act
d. Decision making

15. _________ describes how content an individual is with his or her job.

The happier people are within their job, the more satisfied they are said to be. _________ is not the same as motivation, although it is clearly linked.

a. Goal-setting theory
b. Human relations
c. Job analysis
d. Job Satisfaction

16. _________ are a special type of work behavior that are defined as individual behaviors that are beneficial to the organization and are discretionary, not directly or explicitly recognized by the formal reward system. These behaviors are rather a matter of personal choice, such that their omission are not generally understood as punishable. _________ are thought to have an important impact on the effectiveness and efficiency of work teams and organizations, therefore contributing to the overall productivity of the organization.
a. Organizational citizenship behaviors
b. A Stake in the Outcome
c. AAAI
d. A4e

17. A _________ is a research instrument consisting of a series of questions and other prompts for the purpose of gathering information from respondents. Although they are often designed for statistical analysis of the responses, this is not always the case. The _________ was invented by Sir Francis Galton.
a. Questionnaire construction
b. Questionnaire
c. Mystery shoppers
d. Structured interview

18. In politics, a _________, (by metaphor with the carved _________ at the prow of a sailing ship), is a person who holds an important title or office yet executes little actual power, most commonly limited by convention rather than law. Common _________s include constitutional monarchs, such as: Queen Elizabeth II, the Emperor of Japan, or presidents in parliamentary democracies, such as the President of Israel.

While the authority of a _________ is in practice generally symbolic, public opinion, respect for the office or the office holder and access to high levels of government can give them significant influence on events.

a. 33 Strategies of War
b. 1990 Clean Air Act
c. 28-hour day
d. Figurehead

19. _________ is purposeful and reflective judgment about what to believe or what to do in response to observations, experience, verbal or written expressions, or arguments. _________ might involve determining the meaning and significance of what is observed or expressed, or, concerning a given inference or argument, determining whether there is adequate justification to accept the conclusion as true. Hence, Fisher ' Scriven define _________ as 'Skilled, active, interpretation and evaluation of observations, communications, information, and argumentation.' Parker ' Moore define it more narrowly as the careful, deliberate determination of whether one should accept, reject, or suspend judgment about a claim and the degree of confidence with which one accepts or rejects it.

a. Risk management
b. Kanban
c. Virtual team
d. Critical thinking

20. _________ , often measured as an _________ Quotient (EQ), is a term that describes the ability, capacity, skill or (in the case of the trait _________ model) a self-perceived ability, to identify, assess, and manage the emotions of one's self, of others, and of groups. Different models have been proposed for the definition of _________ and disagreement exists as to how the term should be used. Despite these disagreements, which are often highly technical, the ability _________ and trait _________ models (but not the mixed models) are enjoying considerable support in the literature and have successful applications in many different domains.

a. AAAI
b. A Stake in the Outcome
c. A4e
d. Emotional intelligence

21. _________ is the pursuit of influencing outcomes -- including public-policy and resource allocation decisions within political, economic, and social systems and institutions -- that directly affect people's current lives. (Cohen, 2001)

Therefore, _________ can be seen as a deliberate process of speaking out on issues of concern in order to exert some influence on behalf of ideas or persons. Based on this definition, Cohen (2001) states that 'ideologues of all persuasions advocate' to bring a change in people's lives.

a. AAAI
b. Advocacy
c. A Stake in the Outcome
d. A4e

22. In a military context, the _________ is the line of authority and responsibility along which orders are passed within a military unit and between different units. The term is also used in a civilian management context describing comparable hierarchical structures of authority.

a. 28-hour day
b. 1990 Clean Air Act
c. French leave
d. Chain of command

23. An _________ is a meeting that official bodies, and associations involving the public, are often required by law to hold.

An _________ is generally held every year to inform their members of previous and future activities. It is an opportunity for the shareholders and partners to receive copies of the company's accounts as well as reviewing fiscal information for the past year and asking any questions regarding the decisions the business will take in the future.

a. A4e
b. AAAI
c. A Stake in the Outcome
d. Annual general meeting

24. _________ has become one of the most popular theories in organizational psychology.

Goal setting has been a formula used for acheivement since the early 1800s. The form and pattern has cahanged drastically over the years and there is still much debate as to what is the most efective pattern to follow.

a. Human relations
b. Job satisfaction
c. Corporate Culture
d. Goal-setting theory

25. _________ is a business magazine published by McGraw-Hill. It was first published in 1929 (as The Business Week) under the direction of Malcolm Muir, who was serving as president of the McGraw-Hill Publishing company at the time. Its primary competitors in the national business magazine category are Fortune and Forbes, which are published bi-weekly.
a. Democracy in America
b. The Wealth of Nations
c. Hotel Vikas
d. BusinessWeek

26. _________ has been described as the 'process of social influence in which one person can enlist the aid and support of others in the accomplishment of a common task' . A definition more inclusive of followers comes from Alan Keith of Genentech who said '_________ is ultimately about creating a way for people to contribute to making something extraordinary happen.'

_________ is one of the most salient aspects of the organizational context. However, defining _________ has been challenging.

a. 1990 Clean Air Act
b. Situational leadership
c. 28-hour day
d. Leadership

1. The _________ of 2002 (Pub.L. 107-204, 116 Stat. 745, enacted July 30, 2002), also known as the Public Company Accounting Reform and Investor Protection Act of 2002 and commonly called Sarbanes-Oxley, Sarbox or SOX, is a United States federal law enacted on July 30, 2002, as a reaction to a number of major corporate and accounting scandals including those affecting Enron, Tyco International, Adelphia, Peregrine Systems and WorldCom.

a. Fair Labor Standards Act
b. Sarbanes-Oxley Act of 2002
c. Sarbanes-Oxley Act
d. Letter of credit

2. The 'business case for _________', theorizes that in a global marketplace, a company that employs a diverse workforce (both men and women, people of many generations, people from ethnically and racially diverse backgrounds etc.) is better able to understand the demographics of the marketplace it serves and is thus better equipped to thrive in that marketplace than a company that has a more limited range of employee demographics.

An additional corollary suggests that a company that supports the _________ of its workforce can also improve employee satisfaction, productivity and retention.

a. Trademark
b. Diversity
c. Virtual team
d. Kanban

3. An _________ is a situation that will often involve an apparent conflict between moral imperatives, in which to obey one would result in transgressing another. This is also called an ethical paradox since in moral philosophy, paradox plays a central role in ethics debates. For instance, an ethical admonition to 'love thy neighbour as thy self' is not always just in contrast with, but sometimes in contradiction to an armed neighbour actively trying to kill you: if he or she succeeds, you will not be able to love him or her.

a. AAAI
b. Ethical dilemma
c. A Stake in the Outcome
d. A4e

4. _________ can be regarded as an outcome of mental processes (cognitive process) leading to the selection of a course of action among several alternatives. Every _________ process produces a final choice. The output can be an action or an opinion of choice.

a. 1990 Clean Air Act
b. Decision making
c. 33 Strategies of War
d. 28-hour day

5. _________ is an increasingly broadening term with which an organization, or other human system describes the combination of traditionally administrative personnel functions with acquisition and application of skills, knowledge and experience, Employee Relations and resource planning at various levels. The field draws upon concepts developed in Industrial/Organizational Psychology and System Theory. _________ has at least two related interpretations depending on context. The original usage derives from political economy and economics, where it was traditionally called labor, one of four factors of production although this perspective is changing as a function of new and ongoing research into more strategic approaches at national levels. This first usage is used more in terms of '_________ development', and can go beyond just organizations to the level of nations . The more traditional usage within corporations and businesses refers to the individuals within a firm or agency, and to the portion of the organization that deals with hiring, firing, training, and other personnel issues, typically referred to as `_________ management'.

a. Progressive discipline
b. Human resource management
c. Bradford Factor
d. Human resources

6. An _________ is any party that makes an investment.

The term has taken on a specific meaning in finance to describe the particular types of people and companies that regularly purchase equity or debt securities for financial gain in exchange for funding an expanding company. Less frequently, the term is applied to parties who purchase real estate, currency, commodity derivatives, personal property, or other assets.

a. A Stake in the Outcome
b. AAAI
c. Investor
d. A4e

7. _________ refers to various methodologies for analyzing the requirements of a job.

The general purpose of _________ is to document the requirements of a job and the work performed. Job and task analysis is performed as a basis for later improvements, including: definition of a job domain; describing a job; developing performance appraisals, selection systems, promotion criteria, training needs assessment, and compensation plans.

a. Management process
b. Work design
c. Hersey-Blanchard situational theory
d. Job analysis

8. A mutual shareholder or _________ is an individual or company (including a corporation) that legally owns one or more shares of stock in a joint stock company. A company's shareholders collectively own that company. Thus, the typical goal of such companies is to enhance shareholder value.

a. 1990 Clean Air Act
b. Shareholder
c. Free riding
d. Stockholder

9. A chief executive officer (_________) or chief executive is one of the highest-ranking corporate officer (executive) or administrator in charge of total management. An individual selected as President and _________ of a corporation, company, organization, or agency, reports to the board of directors. In internal communication and press releases, many companies capitalize the term and those of other high positions, even when they are not proper nouns.

a. Director of communications
b. Portfolio manager
c. Chief executive officer
d. CEO

10. In a military context, the _________ is the line of authority and responsibility along which orders are passed within a military unit and between different units. The term is also used in a civilian management context describing comparable hierarchical structures of authority.

a. 1990 Clean Air Act
b. French leave
c. 28-hour day
d. Chain of command

11. _________ is how top executives of business corporations are paid. This includes a basic salary, bonuses, shares, options and other company benefits. Over the past three decades, _________ has risen dramatically beyond the rising levels of an average worker's wage.

a. Association management company
b. Evidence-based management
c. Anti-leadership
d. Executive compensation

12. _________ is one of the managerial functions like planning, organizing, staffing and directing. It is an important function because it helps to check the errors and to take the corrective action so that deviation from standards are minimized and stated goals of the organization are achieved in desired manner.According to modern concepts, _________ is a foreseeing action whereas earlier concept of _________ was used only when errors were detected. _________ in management means setting standards, measuring actual performance and taking corrective action.

a. Turnover
b. Schedule of reinforcement
c. Control
d. Decision tree pruning

13. _________ is an inventory strategy that strives to improve the return on investment of a business by reducing in-process inventory and its associated carrying costs. To meet _________ objectives, the process relies on signals between different points in the process. This means the process is often driven by a series of signals, or Kanban , which tell production when to make the next part. Kanban are usually 'tickets' but can be simple visual signals, such as the presence or absence of a part on a shelf. Implemented correctly, _________ can dramatically improve a manufacturing organization's return on investment, quality, and efficiency.
a. 1990 Clean Air Act
b. Just-in-time
c. 33 Strategies of War
d. 28-hour day

14. A _________ is typically described as a deliberate plan of action to guide decisions and achieve rational outcome(s.) However, the term may also be used to denote what is actually done, even though it is unplanned.

The term may apply to government, private sector organizations and groups, and individuals.

a. 33 Strategies of War
b. Policy
c. 1990 Clean Air Act
d. 28-hour day

15. _________ is unwelcome harassment of a sexual nature, or based upon the receiving party's sex or gender. In some contexts or circumstances, _________ may be illegal. It includes a range of behavior from seemingly mild transgressions and annoyances to actual sexual abuse or sexual assault.
a. Hypernorms
b. 1990 Clean Air Act
c. Sexual harassment
d. 28-hour day

16. _________ is an idea in the field of Organizational studies and management which describes the psychology, attitudes, experiences, beliefs and Values (personal and cultural values) of an organization. It has been defined as 'the specific collection of values and norms that are shared by people and groups in an organization and that control the way they interact with each other and with stakeholders outside the organization.'

This definition continues to explain organizational values also known as 'beliefs and ideas about what kinds of goals members of an organization should pursue and ideas about the appropriate kinds or standards of behavior organizational members should use to achieve these goals. From organizational values develop organizational norms, guidelines or expectations that prescribe appropriate kinds of behavior by employees in particular situations and control the behavior of organizational members towards one another.'

_________ is not the same as corporate culture.

a. Union shop
b. Organizational development
c. Organizational effectiveness
d. Organizational culture

17. In economics, the term _________ refers to situations where the advancement of a qualified person within the hierarchy of an organization is stopped at a lower level because of some form of discrimination, most commonly sexism or racism, but since the term was coined, '_________' has also come to describe the limited advancement of the deaf, blind, disabled, aged and sexual minorities.It is an unofficial, invisible barrier that prevents women and minorities from advancing in businesses.

This situation is referred to as a 'ceiling' as there is a limitation blocking upward advancement, and 'glass' (transparent) because the limitation is not immediately apparent and is normally an unwritten and unofficial policy. This invisible barrier continues to exist, even though there are no explicit obstacles keeping minorities from acquiring advanced job positions - there are no advertisements that specifically say 'no minorities hired at this establishment', nor are there any formal orders that say 'minorities are not qualified' - but they do lie beneath the surface.

a. 28-hour day
b. 1990 Clean Air Act
c. 33 Strategies of War
d. Glass ceiling

18. The _________ of 1967, Pub. L. No. 90-202, 81 Stat. 602 (Dec. 15, 1967), codified as Chapter 14 of Title 29 of the United States Code, 29 U.S.C. Â§ 621 through 29 U.S.C. Â§ 634 (ADEA), prohibits employment discrimination against persons 40 years of age or older in the United States). The law also sets standards for pensions and benefits provided by employers and requires that information about the needs of older workers be provided to the general public.

a. Unemployment and Farm Relief Act
b. Extra time
c. Age Discrimination in Employment Act
d. Undue hardship

19. _________ is a contract between two parties, one being the employer and the other being the employee. An employee may be defined as: 'A person in the service of another under any contract of hire, express or implied, oral or written, where the employer has the power or right to control and direct the employee in the material details of how the work is to be performed.' Black's Law Dictionary page 471 (5th ed. 1979.)
a. Employment
b. Employment rate
c. Employment counsellor
d. Exit interview

20. The _________ 1970 is an Act of the United Kingdom Parliament which prohibits any less favourable treatment between men and women in terms of pay and conditions of employment. It came into force on 29 December 1975. The term pay is interpreted in a broad sense to include, on top of wages, things like holidays, pension rights, company perks and some kinds of bonuses.
a. Australian labour law
b. Equal Pay Act
c. Oncale v. Sundowner Offshore Services
d. Architectural Barriers Act of 1968

21. _________ occurs when expectant women are fired, not hired, or otherwise discriminated against due to their pregnancy or intention to become pregnant. Common forms of _________ include not being hired due to visible pregnancy or likelihood of becoming pregnant, being fired after informing an employer of one's pregnancy, being fired after maternity leave, and receiving a pay dock due to pregnancy. In the United States, since 1978, employers are legally bound to provide what insurance, leave pay, and additional support that would be bestowed upon any employee with medical leave or disability.
a. 28-hour day
b. Pregnancy Discrimination
c. 1990 Clean Air Act
d. 33 Strategies of War

22. An _________ is a person who has possession of an enterprise and assumes significant accountability for the inherent risks and the outcome. It is an ambitious leader who combines land, labor, and capital to create and market new goods or services. The term is a loanword from French and was first defined by the Irish economist Richard Cantillon.

a. A4e
b. AAAI
c. A Stake in the Outcome
d. Entrepreneur

23. In politics, a _________, (by metaphor with the carved _________ at the prow of a sailing ship), is a person who holds an important title or office yet executes little actual power, most commonly limited by convention rather than law. Common _________s include constitutional monarchs, such as: Queen Elizabeth II, the Emperor of Japan, or presidents in parliamentary democracies, such as the President of Israel.

While the authority of a _________ is in practice generally symbolic, public opinion, respect for the office or the office holder and access to high levels of government can give them significant influence on events.

a. 33 Strategies of War
b. Figurehead
c. 1990 Clean Air Act
d. 28-hour day

24. In a human resources context, _________ or labor _________ is the rate at which an employer gains and loses employees. Simple ways to describe it are 'how long employees tend to stay' or 'the rate of traffic through the revolving door.' _________ is measured for individual companies and for their industry as a whole. If an employer is said to have a high _________ relative to its competitors, it means that employees of that company have a shorter average tenure than those of other companies in the same industry.

a. Career portfolios
b. Ten year occupational employment projection
c. Continuous
d. Turnover

25. A _________ exists when an employee experiences workplace harassment and fears going to work because of the offensive, intimidating religion, sex, national origin, age, disability, veteran status, or, in some jurisdictions, sexual orientation, political affiliation, citizenship status, marital status, or personal appearance. _________ is also one of the two legal categories of sexual harassment.

The anti-discrimination statutes governing _________ are not a general civility code.

a. Contrat nouvelle embauche
b. Financial Security Law of France
c. Flextime
d. Hostile work environment

26. _________ indicates a more-or-less equal exchange or substitution of goods or services. English speakers often use the term to mean 'a favour for a favour' and the phrases with almost identical meaning include: 'what for what,' 'give and take,' 'tit for tat', 'this for that', and 'you scratch my back, and I'll scratch yours'.

In legal usage, _________ indicates that an item or a service has been traded in return for something of value, usually when the propriety or equity of the transaction is in question.

a. 28-hour day
b. 33 Strategies of War
c. 1990 Clean Air Act
d. Quid pro quo

27. _________ is a business magazine published by McGraw-Hill. It was first published in 1929 (as The Business Week) under the direction of Malcolm Muir, who was serving as president of the McGraw-Hill Publishing company at the time. Its primary competitors in the national business magazine category are Fortune and Forbes, which are published bi-weekly.
a. Democracy in America
b. The Wealth of Nations
c. Hotel Vikas
d. BusinessWeek

1. An _________ is a mostly hierarchical concept of subordination of entities that collaborate and contribute to serve one common aim.

Organizations are a variant of clustered entities. The structure of an organization is usually set up in many a styles, dependent on their objectives and ambience.

a. Organizational development
b. Organizational structure
c. Open shop
d. Informal organization

2. _________ is a strategic planning method used to evaluate the Strengths, Weaknesses, Opportunities, and Threats involved in a project or in a business venture. It involves specifying the objective of the business venture or project and identifying the internal and external factors that are favorable and unfavorable to achieving that objective. The technique is credited to Albert Humphrey, who led a convention at Stanford University in the 1960s and 1970s using data from Fortune 500 companies.
a. Corporate image
b. Marketing
c. SWOT analysis
d. Market share

3. _________ can be regarded as an outcome of mental processes (cognitive process) leading to the selection of a course of action among several alternatives. Every _________ process produces a final choice. The output can be an action or an opinion of choice.
a. 33 Strategies of War
b. 1990 Clean Air Act
c. 28-hour day
d. Decision making

4. _________ or _________ data refers to selected population characteristics as used in government, marketing or opinion research, or the _________ profiles used in such research. Note the distinction from the term 'demography' Commonly-used _________s include race, age, income, disabilities, mobility (in terms of travel time to work or number of vehicles available), educational attainment, home ownership, employment status, and even location.
a. Affiliation
b. Demographic
c. Abraham Harold Maslow
d. Adam Smith

5. The field of _________ looks at the relationship between management and workers, particularly groups of workers represented by a union.

_________ is an important factor in analyzing 'varieties of capitalism', such as neocorporatism, social democracy, and neoliberalism

a. Informal organization
b. Overtime
c. Industrial relations
d. Organizational effectiveness

6. In mainstream economic theories, the supply of labor is the number of total hours that workers wish to work at a given real wage rate. Realisticly, the _________ is a fuction of various factors within an economy. For instance, overpopulation increases the number of available workers driving down wages and can result in high unemployment.
a. 1990 Clean Air Act
b. 28-hour day
c. 33 Strategies of War
d. Labor supply

7. _________ is subcontracting a process, such as product design or manufacturing, to a third-party company. The decision to outsource is often made in the interest of lowering cost or making better use of time and energy costs, redirecting or conserving energy directed at the competencies of a particular business, or to make more efficient use of land, labor, capital, (information) technology and resources. _________ became part of the business lexicon during the 1980s.
a. Unemployment insurance
b. Opinion leadership
c. Outsourcing
d. Operant conditioning

8. A _________ is the system of organizations, people, technology, activities, information and resources involved in moving a product or service from supplier to customer. _________ activities transform natural resources, raw materials and components into a finished product that is delivered to the end customer. In sophisticated _________ systems, used products may re-enter the _________ at any point where residual value is recyclable.
a. Wholesalers
b. Packaging
c. Drop shipping
d. Supply chain

9. _________ is the management of a network of interconnected businesses involved in the ultimate provision of product and service packages required by end customers (Harland, 1996.) _________ spans all movement and storage of raw materials, work-in-process inventory, and finished goods from point of origin to point of consumption (supply chain.)

The definition an American professional association put forward is that _________ encompasses the planning and management of all activities involved in sourcing, procurement, conversion, and logistics management activities.

a. Packaging
b. Freight forwarder
c. Drop shipping
d. Supply chain management

10. _________ is one of the four elements of marketing mix. An organization or set of organizations (go-betweens) involved in the process of making a product or service available for use or consumption by a consumer or business user.

The other three parts of the marketing mix are product, pricing, and promotion.

a. Missing completely at random
b. Job creation programs
c. Distribution
d. Matching theory

11. _________ is an idea in the field of Organizational studies and management which describes the psychology, attitudes, experiences, beliefs and Values (personal and cultural values) of an organization. It has been defined as 'the specific collection of values and norms that are shared by people and groups in an organization and that control the way they interact with each other and with stakeholders outside the organization.'

This definition continues to explain organizational values also known as 'beliefs and ideas about what kinds of goals members of an organization should pursue and ideas about the appropriate kinds or standards of behavior organizational members should use to achieve these goals. From organizational values develop organizational norms, guidelines or expectations that prescribe appropriate kinds of behavior by employees in particular situations and control the behavior of organizational members towards one another.'

_________ is not the same as corporate culture.

a. Organizational effectiveness
b. Union shop
c. Organizational development
d. Organizational culture

12. In economics and especially in the theory of competition, _________ are obstacles in the path of a firm that make it difficult to enter a given market.

_________ are the source of a firm's pricing power - the ability of a firm to raise prices without losing all its customers.

The term refers to hindrances that an individual may face while trying to gain entrance into a profession or trade.

a. 28-hour day
b. 1990 Clean Air Act
c. Predatory pricing
d. Barriers to entry

13. _________, in microeconomics, are the cost advantages that a business obtains due to expansion. They are factors that cause a producer's average cost per unit to fall as scale is increased. _________ is a long run concept and refers to reductions in unit cost as the size of a facility, or scale, increases.

a. A4e
b. Economies of scale
c. Economies of scope
d. A Stake in the Outcome

14. A _________ is a name or trademark connected with a product or producer. _________s have become increasingly important components of culture and the economy, now being described as 'cultural accessories and personal philosophies'.

Some people distinguish the psychological aspect of a _________ from the experiential aspect.

a. Brand awareness
b. Brand loyalty
c. Brand extension
d. Brand

15. _________, in marketing, consists of a consumer's commitment to repurchase or otherwise continue using the brand and can be demonstrated by repeated buying of a product or service or other positive behaviors such as word of mouth advocacy.

_________ is more than simple repurchasing, however. Customers may repurchase a brand due to situational constraints, a lack of viable alternatives, or out of convenience.

a. Brand awareness
b. Brand extension
c. Brand image
d. Brand loyalty

16. In a military context, the _________ is the line of authority and responsibility along which orders are passed within a military unit and between different units. The term is also used in a civilian management context describing comparable hierarchical structures of authority.
a. French leave
b. 28-hour day
c. 1990 Clean Air Act
d. Chain of command

17. _________ is the removal or simplification of government rules and regulations that constrain the operation of market forces. _________ does not mean elimination of laws against fraud, but eliminating or reducing government control of how business is done, thereby moving toward a more free market.

The stated rationale for '_________' is often that fewer and simpler regulations will lead to a raised level of competitiveness, therefore higher productivity, more efficiency and lower prices overall.

a. Natural rate of unemployment
b. Value added
c. Rehn-Meidner Model
d. Deregulation

18. _________ is the incidence or process of transferring ownership of a business, enterprise, agency or public service from the public sector (government) to the private sector (business.) In a broader sense, _________ refers to transfer of any government function to the private sector including governmental functions like revenue collection and law enforcement.

a. 1990 Clean Air Act
b. 28-hour day
c. Performance reports
d. Privatization

19. In queueing theory, _________ is the proportion of the system's resources which is used by the traffic which arrives at it. It should be strictly less than one for the system to function well. It is usually represented by the symbol ρ.
a. A4e
b. AAAI
c. A Stake in the Outcome
d. Utilization

20. _________ is a type of trade policy that allows traders to act and transact without interference from government. Thus, the policy permits trading partners mutual gains from trade, with goods and services produced according to the theory of comparative advantage.

Under a _________ policy, prices are a reflection of true supply and demand, and are the sole determinant of resource allocation.

a. 1990 Clean Air Act
b. 28-hour day
c. Free Trade
d. 33 Strategies of War

21. _________ is a designated group of countries that have agreed to eliminate tariffs, quotas and preferences on most (if not all) goods and services traded between them. It can be considered the second stage of economic integration. Countries choose this kind of economic integration form if their economical structures are complementary.
a. 28-hour day
b. 33 Strategies of War
c. 1990 Clean Air Act
d. Free trade area

22. The _________ was the outcome of the failure of negotiating governments to create the International Trade Organization (ITO.) GATT was formed in 1947 and lasted until 1994, when it was replaced by the World Trade Organization. The Bretton Woods Conference had introduced the idea for an organization to regulate trade as part of a larger plan for economic recovery after World War II.

a. General Agreement on Tariffs and Trade
b. Multilateral treaty
c. 28-hour day
d. 1990 Clean Air Act

23. The _________ is a trilateral trade bloc in North America created by the governments of the United States, Canada, and Mexico. The agreement creating the trade bloc came into force on January 1, 1994. It superseded the Canada-United States Free Trade Agreement between the U.S. and Canada.

a. Trade union
b. Business war game
c. North American Free Trade Agreement
d. Career portfolios

24. A _________ is a general term that describes any government policy or regulation that restricts international trade. The barriers can take many forms, including the following terms that include many restrictions in international trade within multiple countries that import and export any items of trade.

- Import duty
- Import licenses
- Export licenses
- Import quotas
- Tariffs
- Subsidies
- Non-tariff barriers to trade
- Voluntary Export Restraints
- Local Content Requirements
- Embargo

Most _________s work on the same principle: the imposition of some sort of cost on trade that raises the price of the traded products. If two or more nations repeatedly use _________s against each other, then a trade war results.

a. Customs brokerage
b. Trade creation
c. Most favoured nation
d. Trade barrier

25. The _________ is an international organization designed by its founders to supervise and liberalize international trade. The organization officially commenced on 1 January 1995, under the Marrakesh Agreement, succeeding the 1947 General Agreement on Tariffs and Trade (GATT.)

The _________ deals with regulation of trade between participating countries; it provides a framework for negotiating and formalising trade agreements, and a dispute resolution process aimed at enforcing participants' adherence to _________ agreements which are signed by representatives of member governments and ratified by their parliaments.

a. Network planning and design
b. 1990 Clean Air Act
c. World Trade Organization
d. National Institute for Occupational Safety and Health

26. _________, commonly known as e-commerce, consists of the buying and selling of products or services over electronic systems such as the Internet and other computer networks. The amount of trade conducted electronically has grown extraordinarily with widespread Internet usage. The use of commerce is conducted in this way, spurring and drawing on innovations in electronic funds transfer, supply chain management, Internet marketing, online transaction processing, electronic data interchange (EDI), inventory management systems, and automated data collection systems.
a. Online shopping
b. A Stake in the Outcome
c. A4e
d. Electronic Commerce

27. _________ is a term used to describe any moral, political that stresses human interdependence and the importance of a collective, rather than the importance of separate individuals. Collectivists focus on community and society, and seek to give priority to group goals over individual goals. The philosophical underpinnings of _________ are for some related to holism or organicism - the view that the whole is greater than the sum of its parts/pieces.
a. 1990 Clean Air Act
b. 28-hour day
c. Collectivism
d. Collaborative methods

28. _________ is a business magazine published by McGraw-Hill. It was first published in 1929 (as The Business Week) under the direction of Malcolm Muir, who was serving as president of the McGraw-Hill Publishing company at the time. Its primary competitors in the national business magazine category are Fortune and Forbes, which are published bi-weekly.
a. Democracy in America
b. Hotel Vikas
c. BusinessWeek
d. The Wealth of Nations

29. The _________ is a general business term describing the largest group of consumers for a specified industry product. It is the opposite extreme of the term niche market.

The _________ is the group of consumers who occupy the overwhelming mass of a bell curve for common household products, i.e. they could be tagged as being 'average'.

a. Chief legal officer
b. Chief analytics officer
c. Supervisory board
d. Mass market

30. _________ has been described as the 'process of social influence in which one person can enlist the aid and support of others in the accomplishment of a common task' . A definition more inclusive of followers comes from Alan Keith of Genentech who said '_________ is ultimately about creating a way for people to contribute to making something extraordinary happen.'

_________ is one of the most salient aspects of the organizational context. However, defining _________ has been challenging.

a. Situational leadership
b. Leadership
c. 1990 Clean Air Act
d. 28-hour day

31. _________ is the corporate management term for the act of reorganizing the legal, ownership, operational, or other structures of a company for the purpose of making it more profitable, or better organized for its present needs. Alternate reasons for _________ include a change of ownership or ownership structure, demerger repositioning debt _________ and financial _________.

a. Net worth
b. Market value
c. Market value added
d. Restructuring

1. _________ can be regarded as an outcome of mental processes (cognitive process) leading to the selection of a course of action among several alternatives. Every _________ process produces a final choice. The output can be an action or an opinion of choice.

a. 33 Strategies of War
b. Decision making
c. 28-hour day
d. 1990 Clean Air Act

2. _________ is one of the managerial functions like planning, organizing, staffing and directing. It is an important function because it helps to check the errors and to take the corrective action so that deviation from standards are minimized and stated goals of the organization are achieved in desired manner.According to modern concepts, _________ is a foreseeing action whereas earlier concept of _________ was used only when errors were detected. _________ in management means setting standards, measuring actual performance and taking corrective action.

a. Schedule of reinforcement
b. Control
c. Decision tree pruning
d. Turnover

3. _________ is a concept based on the fact that rationality of individuals is limited by the information they have, the cognitive limitations of their minds, and the finite amount of time they have to make decisions. This contrasts with the concept of rationality as optimization. Another way to look at _________ is that, because decision-makers lack the ability and resources to arrive at the optimal solution, they instead apply their rationality only after having greatly simplified the choices available.

a. Mixed strategy
b. Transferable utility
c. Bounded rationality
d. Complete information

4. In economics, business, retail, and accounting, a _________ is the value of money that has been used up to produce something, and hence is not available for use anymore. In economics, a _________ is an alternative that is given up as a result of a decision. In business, the _________ may be one of acquisition, in which case the amount of money expended to acquire it is counted as _________.

a. Fixed costs
b. Cost overrun
c. Cost allocation
d. Cost

5. In decision theory and estimation theory, the _________ of an estimator, $\hat{\theta}$, of an unknown parameter of the distribution, θ, is the expected value of the loss function

$$R(\theta,\hat{\theta}) = \mathbb{E}_\theta L(\theta,\hat{\theta}) = \int L(\theta,\hat{\theta})\, dP_\theta.$$

where dP_θ is a probability measure parametrized by θ.

- For a scalar parameter θ and a quadratic loss function,

  $$L(\theta,\hat{\theta}) = (\theta - \hat{\theta})^2$$

  the _________ function becomes the mean squared error of the estimate,

  $$R(\theta,\hat{\theta}) = E_\theta(\theta - \hat{\theta})^2$$

- In density estimation, the unknown parameter is probability density itself. The loss function is typically chosen to be a norm in an appropriate function space. For example, for L^2 norm,

  $$L(f,\hat{f}) = \|f - \hat{f}\|_2^2$$

  the _________ function becomes the mean integrated squared error

  $$R(f,\hat{f}) = E\|f - \hat{f}\|^2$$

.

a. Linear model
b. Risk aversion
c. Risk
d. Financial modeling

6. _________ of the learning curve effect and the closely related experience curve effect express the relationship between equations for experience and efficiency or between efficiency gains and investment in the effort. The experience of 'learning curves' was first observed by the 19th Century German psychologist Hermann Ebbinghaus according to the difficulty of memorizing varying numbers of verbal stimuli, and subsequent learning about the complex processes of learning are discussed in the

.

The rule used for representing the learning curve effect states that the more times a task has been performed, the less time will be required on each subsequent iteration.

a. Distribution
b. Spatial Decision Support Systems
c. Models
d. Point biserial correlation coefficient

7. The term _________ is used in various contexts. For example, in business process modeling the enterprise _________ is often referred to as the business _________. Process models are core concepts in the discipline of Process Engineering.
a. Process model
b. 1990 Clean Air Act
c. 33 Strategies of War
d. 28-hour day

8. _________ describes the situation when output from (or information about the result of) an event or phenomenon in the past will influence the same event/phenomenon in the present or future. When an event is part of a chain of cause-and-effect that forms a circuit or loop, then the event is said to 'feed back' into itself.

_________ is also a synonym for:

- _________ signal; the information about the initial event that is the basis for subsequent modification of the event.
- _________ loop; the causal path that leads from the initial generation of the _________ signal to the subsequent modification of the event.

_________ is a mechanism, process or signal that is looped back to control a system within itself. Such a loop is called a _________ loop.

a. 1990 Clean Air Act
b. Feedback
c. Positive feedback
d. Feedback loop

9. A chief executive officer (_________) or chief executive is one of the highest-ranking corporate officer (executive) or administrator in charge of total management. An individual selected as President and _________ of a corporation, company, organization, or agency, reports to the board of directors. In internal communication and press releases, many companies capitalize the term and those of other high positions, even when they are not proper nouns.

a. Director of communications
b. Chief executive officer
c. CEO
d. Portfolio manager

10. _________ is an idea in the field of Organizational studies and management which describes the psychology, attitudes, experiences, beliefs and Values (personal and cultural values) of an organization. It has been defined as 'the specific collection of values and norms that are shared by people and groups in an organization and that control the way they interact with each other and with stakeholders outside the organization.'

This definition continues to explain organizational values also known as 'beliefs and ideas about what kinds of goals members of an organization should pursue and ideas about the appropriate kinds or standards of behavior organizational members should use to achieve these goals. From organizational values develop organizational norms, guidelines or expectations that prescribe appropriate kinds of behavior by employees in particular situations and control the behavior of organizational members towards one another.'

_________ is not the same as corporate culture.

a. Union shop
b. Organizational development
c. Organizational effectiveness
d. Organizational culture

11. _________ consists of the mental process of thinking involved with the process of judging the merits of multiple options and selecting one of them for action. Some simple examples include deciding whether to get up in the morning or go back to sleep, or selecting a given route for a journey. More complex examples (often decisions that affect what a person thinks or their core beliefs) include choosing a lifestyle, religious affiliation, or political position.
a. Championship mobilization
b. Groups decision making
c. Trade study
d. Choice

12. _________ is decision making in groups consisting of multiple members/entities. The challenge of group decision is deciding what action a group should take. There are various systems designed to solve this problem.
a. Control of Substances Hazardous to Health Regulations 2002
b. Groups decision making
c. Collaborative Planning, Forecasting and Replenishment
d. Genbutsu

13. _________ is a type of thought exhibited by group members who try to minimize conflict and reach consensus without critically testing, analyzing, and evaluating ideas. Individual creativity, uniqueness, and independent thinking are lost in the pursuit of group cohesiveness, as are the advantages of reasonable balance in choice and thought that might normally be obtained by making decisions as a group. During _________, members of the group avoid promoting viewpoints outside the comfort zone of consensus thinking.

a. Psychological statistics
b. Diffusion of responsibility
c. Groupthink
d. Self-report inventory

14. The 'business case for _________', theorizes that in a global marketplace, a company that employs a diverse workforce (both men and women, people of many generations, people from ethnically and racially diverse backgrounds etc.) is better able to understand the demographics of the marketplace it serves and is thus better equipped to thrive in that marketplace than a company that has a more limited range of employee demographics.

An additional corollary suggests that a company that supports the _________ of its workforce can also improve employee satisfaction, productivity and retention.

a. Trademark
b. Virtual team
c. Diversity
d. Kanban

15. A _________ is the term given to a company that facilitates the learning of its members and continuously transforms itself. _________s develop as a result of the pressures facing modern organizations and enables them to remain competitive in the business environment. A _________ has five main features; systems thinking, personal mastery, mental models, shared vision and team learning.

a. Hoshin Kanri
b. Quality function deployment
c. Learning organization
d. 1990 Clean Air Act

16. _________ is an area of knowledge within organizational theory that studies models and theories about the way an organization learns and adapts.

In Organizational development (OD), learning is a characteristic of an adaptive organization, i.e., an organization that is able to sense changes in signals from its environment (both internal and external) and adapt accordingly.

a. A4e
b. AAAI
c. A Stake in the Outcome
d. Organizational learning

17. _________ is the pursuit of influencing outcomes -- including public-policy and resource allocation decisions within political, economic, and social systems and institutions -- that directly affect people's current lives. (Cohen, 2001)

Therefore, _________ can be seen as a deliberate process of speaking out on issues of concern in order to exert some influence on behalf of ideas or persons. Based on this definition, Cohen (2001) states that 'ideologues of all persuasions advocate' to bring a change in people's lives.

a. AAAI
b. A4e
c. A Stake in the Outcome
d. Advocacy

18. _________ is, in very basic words, a position a firm occupies against its competitors.

According to Michael Porter, the three methods for creating a sustainable _________ are through:

1. Cost leadership

2. Differentiation

3. Focus (economics)

a. 1990 Clean Air Act
b. Theory Z
c. 28-hour day
d. Competitive advantage

19. _________ is any process of estimating or inferring how local policies, actions, or changes influences the state of the neighboring universe. It also can be defined, as an approach to problem solving, as viewing 'problems' as parts of an overall system, rather than reacting to present outcomes or events and potentially contributing to further development of the undesired issue or problem. _________ is a framework that is based on the belief that the component parts of a system can best be understood in the context of relationships with each other and with other systems, rather than in isolation.

a. 28-hour day
b. 1990 Clean Air Act
c. Systems theory
d. Systems thinking

20. In a military context, the _________ is the line of authority and responsibility along which orders are passed within a military unit and between different units. The term is also used in a civilian management context describing comparable hierarchical structures of authority.
a. 1990 Clean Air Act
b. 28-hour day
c. French leave
d. Chain of command

21. _________ is a group creativity technique designed to generate a large number of ideas for the solution of a problem. The method was first popularized in the late 1930s by Alex Faickney Osborn in a book called Applied Imagination. Osborn proposed that groups could double their creative output with _________.
a. Affiliation
b. Abraham Harold Maslow
c. Brainstorming
d. Adam Smith

22. The _________ is a decision making method for use among groups of many sizes, who want to make their decision quickly, as by a vote, but want everyone's opinions taken into account (as opposed to traditional voting, where only the largest group is considered) . The method of tallying is the difference. First, every member of the group gives their view of the solution, with a short explanation.
a. Hierarchical Decision Process
b. Belief decision matrix
c. Decision model
d. Nominal group technique

23. _________ is a common problem in brainstorming groups. It is a tendency for one individual to block or inhibit other people during a group discussion. For example, if six people are in a group and one person is talking about his or her idea, then the other five people are 'blocked' and less able to provide their own creative input.

a. 33 Strategies of War
b. 28-hour day
c. 1990 Clean Air Act
d. Production blocking

24. The _________ is a systematic, interactive forecasting method which relies on a panel of independent experts. The carefully selected experts answer questionnaires in two or more rounds. After each round, a facilitator provides an anonymous summary of the experts' forecasts from the previous round as well as the reasons they provided for their judgments.
a. Quality function deployment
b. Hoshin Kanri
c. Learning organization
d. Delphi method

25. _________ is a business magazine published by McGraw-Hill. It was first published in 1929 (as The Business Week) under the direction of Malcolm Muir, who was serving as president of the McGraw-Hill Publishing company at the time. Its primary competitors in the national business magazine category are Fortune and Forbes, which are published bi-weekly.
a. The Wealth of Nations
b. Hotel Vikas
c. BusinessWeek
d. Democracy in America

1. A _________ is a brief written statement of the purpose of a company or organization. Ideally, a _________ guides the actions of the organization, spells out its overall goal, provides a sense of direction, and guides decision making for all levels of management.

_________s often contain the following:

- Purpose and aim of the organization
- The organization's primary stakeholders: clients, stockholders, etc.
- Responsibilities of the organization toward these stakeholders
- Products and services offered

In developing a _________:

- Encourage as much input as feasible from employees, volunteers, and other stakeholders
- Publicize it broadly

The _________ can be used to resolve differences between business stakeholders. Stakeholders include: employees including managers and executives, stockholders, board of directors, customers, suppliers, distributors, creditors, governments (local, state, federal, etc.), unions, competitors, NGO's, and the general public.

a. 28-hour day
b. 1990 Clean Air Act
c. 33 Strategies of War
d. Mission statement

2. In a military context, the _________ is the line of authority and responsibility along which orders are passed within a military unit and between different units. The term is also used in a civilian management context describing comparable hierarchical structures of authority.
a. Chain of command
b. 1990 Clean Air Act
c. French leave
d. 28-hour day

3. _________ involves establishing specific, measurable and time-targeted objectives. Work on the theory of goal-setting suggests that it's an effective tool for making progress by ensuring that participants in a group with a common goal are clearly aware of what is expected from them if an objective is to be achieved. On a personal level, setting goals is a process that allows people to specify then work towards their own objectives - most commonly with financial or career-based goals.

a. Goal setting
b. Digital strategy
c. Resource-based view
d. Catfish effect

4. A _________ is a list of the general tasks and responsibilities of a position. Typically, it also includes to whom the position reports, specifications such as the qualifications needed by the person in the job, salary range for the position, etc. A _________ is usually developed by conducting a job analysis, which includes examining the tasks and sequences of tasks necessary to perform the job.

a. Job description
b. Recruitment
c. Recruitment advertising
d. Recruitment Process Insourcing

5. An _________ is a mostly hierarchical concept of subordination of entities that collaborate and contribute to serve one common aim.

Organizations are a variant of clustered entities. The structure of an organization is usually set up in many a styles, dependent on their objectives and ambience.

a. Informal organization
b. Organizational development
c. Open shop
d. Organizational structure

6. A _________ is typically described as a deliberate plan of action to guide decisions and achieve rational outcome(s.) However, the term may also be used to denote what is actually done, even though it is unplanned.

The term may apply to government, private sector organizations and groups, and individuals.

a. 1990 Clean Air Act
b. Policy
c. 33 Strategies of War
d. 28-hour day

7. _________ is one of the managerial functions like planning, organizing, staffing and directing. It is an important function because it helps to check the errors and to take the corrective action so that deviation from standards are minimized and stated goals of the organization are achieved in desired manner.According to modern concepts, _________ is a foreseeing action whereas earlier concept of _________ was used only when errors were detected. _________ in management means setting standards, measuring actual performance and taking corrective action.

a. Schedule of reinforcement
b. Decision tree pruning
c. Turnover
d. Control

8. In the fields of science, engineering, industry and statistics, _________ is the degree of closeness of a measured or calculated quantity to its actual (true) value. _________ is closely related to precision, also called reproducibility or repeatability, the degree to which further measurements or calculations show the same or similar results. _________ indicates proximity to the true value, precision to the repeatability or reproducibility of the measurement

The results of calculations or a measurement can be accurate but not precise, precise but not accurate, neither, or both.

a. A4e
b. AAAI
c. A Stake in the Outcome
d. Accuracy

9. _________ is a strategic planning method that some organizations use to make flexible long-term plans. It is in large part an adaptation and generalization of classic methods used by military intelligence.

The original method was that a group of analysts would generate simulation games for policy makers. In business applications, the emphasis on gaming the behavior of opponents was reduced (shifting more toward a game against nature). At Royal Dutch/Shell for example, _________ was viewed as changing mindsets about the exogenous part of the world, prior to formulating specific strategies.

a. Retroactive overtime
b. Time and attendance
c. Labour productivity
d. Scenario planning

10. _________ is a strategic planning method used to evaluate the Strengths, Weaknesses, Opportunities, and Threats involved in a project or in a business venture. It involves specifying the objective of the business venture or project and identifying the internal and external factors that are favorable and unfavorable to achieving that objective. The technique is credited to Albert Humphrey, who led a convention at Stanford University in the 1960s and 1970s using data from Fortune 500 companies.

a. Corporate image
b. Marketing
c. SWOT analysis
d. Market share

11. _________ can be regarded as an outcome of mental processes (cognitive process) leading to the selection of a course of action among several alternatives. Every _________ process produces a final choice. The output can be an action or an opinion of choice.

a. 28-hour day
b. 33 Strategies of War
c. 1990 Clean Air Act
d. Decision making

12. _________, a business term, is a measure of how products and services supplied by a company meet or surpass customer expectation. It is seen as a key performance indicator within business and is part of the four perspectives of a Balanced Scorecard.

In a competitive marketplace where businesses compete for customers, _________ is seen as a key differentiator and increasingly has become a key element of business strategy.

a. Critical Success Factor
b. Customer satisfaction
c. Horizontal integration
d. Foreign ownership

13. _________ concerns all the activities involved in realizing new business opportunities, including product or service design, business model design, and marketing. When splitting business development into two parts, we have: 'business' and 'development'. The first things that come into mind when looking at business are: economics, finance, managerial activities, competition, prices, marketing, etc.

a. 28-hour day
b. 33 Strategies of War
c. 1990 Clean Air Act
d. New business development

14. _________ is the term used to describe a situation where different entities cooperate advantageously for a final outcome. Simply defined, it means that the whole is greater than the sum of the individual parts. Although the whole will be greater than each individual part, this is not the concept of _________.

a. 33 Strategies of War
b. 28-hour day
c. 1990 Clean Air Act
d. Synergy

15. A chief executive officer (_________) or chief executive is one of the highest-ranking corporate officer (executive) or administrator in charge of total management. An individual selected as President and _________ of a corporation, company, organization, or agency, reports to the board of directors. In internal communication and press releases, many companies capitalize the term and those of other high positions, even when they are not proper nouns.

a. Director of communications
b. Portfolio manager
c. CEO
d. Chief executive officer

16. _________ refers to the methods of practicing and using another person's business philosophy. The franchisor grants the independent operator the right to distribute its products, techniques, and trademarks for a percentage of gross monthly sales and a royalty fee. Various tangibles and intangibles such as national or international advertising, training, and other support services are commonly made available by the franchisor.

a. ServiceMaster
b. 28-hour day
c. 1990 Clean Air Act
d. Franchising

17. _________ as defined in business terms is an organization's strategic guide to globalization. A sound _________ should address these questions: what must be (versus what is) the extent of market presence in the world's major markets? How to build the necessary global presence? What must be (versus what is) the optimal locations around the world for the various value chain activities? How to run global presence into global competitive advantage?

Academic research on _________ came of age during the 1980s, including work by Michael Porter and Christopher Bartlett ' Sumantra Ghoshal. Among the forces perceived to bring about the globalization of competition were convergence in economic systems and technological change, especially in information technology, that facilitated and required the coordination of a multinational firm's strategy on a worldwide scale.

a. 33 Strategies of War
b. 28-hour day
c. 1990 Clean Air Act
d. Global strategy

18. _________ is exchange of capital, goods, and services across international borders or territories. In most countries, it represents a significant share of gross domestic product (GDP.) While _________ has been present throughout much of history , its economic, social, and political importance has been on the rise in recent centuries.

a. AAAI
b. A4e
c. A Stake in the Outcome
d. International trade

19. A _________ is an entity formed between two or more parties to undertake economic activity together. The parties agree to create a new entity by both contributing equity, and they then share in the revenues, expenses, and control of the enterprise. The venture can be for one specific project only, or a continuing business relationship such as the Fuji Xerox _________.

a. Patent
b. Civil Rights Act of 1991
c. Meritor Savings Bank v. Vinson
d. Joint venture

20. A _________ is a formal relationship between two or more parties to pursue a set of agreed upon goals or to meet a critical business need while remaining independent organizations.

Partners may provide the _________ with resources such as products, distribution channels, manufacturing capability, project funding, capital equipment, knowledge, expertise, or intellectual property. The alliance is a cooperation or collaboration which aims for a synergy where each partner hopes that the benefits from the alliance will be greater than those from individual efforts.

a. Strategic alliance
b. Process automation
c. Golden parachute
d. Farmshoring

21. An _________ is a person who has possession of an enterprise and assumes significant accountability for the inherent risks and the outcome. It is an ambitious leader who combines land, labor, and capital to create and market new goods or services. The term is a loanword from French and was first defined by the Irish economist Richard Cantillon.

a. AAAI
b. Entrepreneur
c. A Stake in the Outcome
d. A4e

22. In decision theory and estimation theory, the _________ of an estimator, $\hat{\theta}$, of an unknown parameter of the distribution, θ, is the expected value of the loss function

$$R(\theta,\hat{\theta}) = \mathbb{E}_\theta L(\theta,\hat{\theta}) = \int L(\theta,\hat{\theta})\, dP_\theta.$$

where dP_θ is a probability measure parametrized by θ.

- For a scalar parameter θ and a quadratic loss function,

  $$L(\theta,\hat{\theta}) = (\theta - \hat{\theta})^2$$

  the _________ function becomes the mean squared error of the estimate,

  $$R(\theta,\hat{\theta}) = E_\theta(\theta - \hat{\theta})^2$$

- In density estimation, the unknown parameter is probability density itself. The loss function is typically chosen to be a norm in an appropriate function space. For example, for L^2 norm,

  $$L(f,\hat{f}) = \|f - \hat{f}\|_2^2$$

  the _________ function becomes the mean integrated squared error

  $$R(f,\hat{f}) = E\|f - \hat{f}\|^2$$

.

a. Risk aversion
b. Risk
c. Financial modeling
d. Linear model

23. In microeconomics and management, the term _________ describes a style of management control. Vertically integrated companies are united through a hierarchy with a common owner. Usually each member of the hierarchy produces a different product or (market-specific) service, and the products combine to satisfy a common need.

a. Vertical integration
b. 1990 Clean Air Act
c. 28-hour day
d. 33 Strategies of War

24. In economics, business, retail, and accounting, a _________ is the value of money that has been used up to produce something, and hence is not available for use anymore. In economics, a _________ is an alternative that is given up as a result of a decision. In business, the _________ may be one of acquisition, in which case the amount of money expended to acquire it is counted as _________.

a. Cost allocation
b. Cost
c. Fixed costs
d. Cost overrun

25. A _________ is a name or trademark connected with a product or producer. _________s have become increasingly important components of culture and the economy, now being described as 'cultural accessories and personal philosophies'.

Some people distinguish the psychological aspect of a _________ from the experiential aspect.

a. Brand loyalty
b. Brand awareness
c. Brand
d. Brand extension

26. _________ refers to the difference between the cost of materials purchased by a company plus the cost of the labor to assemble a product and the price at which the company sells the product. An example is the price of gasoline at the pump over the price of the oil in it. In national accounts used in macroeconomics, it refers to the contribution of the factors of production, i.e., land, labor, and capital goods, to raising the value of a product and corresponds to the incomes received by the owners of these factors.

a. Minimum wage
b. Deregulation
c. Rehn-Meidner Model
d. Value added

27. _________ is, in very basic words, a position a firm occupies against its competitors.

According to Michael Porter, the three methods for creating a sustainable _________ are through:

1. Cost leadership

2. Differentiation

3. Focus (economics)

a. 1990 Clean Air Act
b. Theory Z
c. 28-hour day
d. Competitive advantage

28. _________ is a business magazine published by McGraw-Hill. It was first published in 1929 (as The Business Week) under the direction of Malcolm Muir, who was serving as president of the McGraw-Hill Publishing company at the time. Its primary competitors in the national business magazine category are Fortune and Forbes, which are published bi-weekly.

a. Hotel Vikas
b. BusinessWeek
c. Democracy in America
d. The Wealth of Nations

29. The _________ Automobile Company is an automobile manufacturer based in Wolfsburg, Germany, and is the original brand within the _________ Group, as well as the largest brand by sales volume.

_________ means 'people's car' in German, in which it is pronounced . Its current tagline or slogan is Das Auto .

a. Turnover
b. Volkswagen
c. Competence-based Strategic Management
d. Rate of return

1. The goal of _________ is to create an organization which will be able to continuously create value for present and future customers, optimizing and organizing it self. Some under _________ understand building blocks which are mandatory for the growth of the organization. To design an organization means to set up a stage where the drama of life will take place.
   a. A Stake in the Outcome
   b. A4e
   c. AAAI
   d. Organizational architecture

2. _________ is a class of behavioural theory that claims that there is no best way to organize a corporation, to lead a company, or to make decisions. Instead, the optimal course of action is contingent (dependant) upon the internal and external situation. Several contingency approaches were developed concurrently in the late 1960s.
   a. Distributed management
   b. Commercial management
   c. Capability management
   d. Contingency theory

3. _________ is an increasingly broadening term with which an organization, or other human system describes the combination of traditionally administrative personnel functions with acquisition and application of skills, knowledge and experience, Employee Relations and resource planning at various levels. The field draws upon concepts developed in Industrial/Organizational Psychology and System Theory. _________ has at least two related interpretations depending on context. The original usage derives from political economy and economics, where it was traditionally called labor, one of four factors of production although this perspective is changing as a function of new and ongoing research into more strategic approaches at national levels. This first usage is used more in terms of '_________ development', and can go beyond just organizations to the level of nations . The more traditional usage within corporations and businesses refers to the individuals within a firm or agency, and to the portion of the organization that deals with hiring, firing, training, and other personnel issues, typically referred to as `_________ management'.
   a. Bradford Factor
   b. Human resources
   c. Human resource management
   d. Progressive discipline

4. An _________ is a mostly hierarchical concept of subordination of entities that collaborate and contribute to serve one common aim.

Organizations are a variant of clustered entities. The structure of an organization is usually set up in many a styles, dependent on their objectives and ambience.

a. Open shop
b. Informal organization
c. Organizational structure
d. Organizational development

5. In a military context, the _________ is the line of authority and responsibility along which orders are passed within a military unit and between different units. The term is also used in a civilian management context describing comparable hierarchical structures of authority.

a. 1990 Clean Air Act
b. French leave
c. 28-hour day
d. Chain of command

6. _________ comprises a range of practices used in an organisation to identify, create, represent, distribute and enable adoption of insights and experiences. Such insights and experiences comprise knowledge, either embodied in individuals or embedded in organisational processes or practice.

An established discipline since 1991 , _________ includes courses taught in the fields of business administration, information systems, management, and library and information sciences .

a. Knowledge management
b. 33 Strategies of War
c. 28-hour day
d. 1990 Clean Air Act

7. _________ refers to various methodologies for analyzing the requirements of a job.

The general purpose of _________ is to document the requirements of a job and the work performed. Job and task analysis is performed as a basis for later improvements, including: definition of a job domain; describing a job; developing performance appraisals, selection systems, promotion criteria, training needs assessment, and compensation plans.

a. Hersey-Blanchard situational theory
b. Work design
c. Management process
d. Job analysis

8. In organizational development (OD), _________ is the application of Socio-Technical Systems principles and techniques to the humanization of work.

The aims of _________ to improved job satisfaction, to improved through-put, to improved quality and to reduced employee problems, e.g., grievances, absenteeism.

Under scientific management people would be directed by reason and the problems of industrial unrest would be appropriately (i.e., scientifically) addressed.

a. Graduate recruitment
b. Management process
c. Path-goal theory
d. Work design

9. _________ refers to increasing the spiritual, political, social or economic strength of individuals and communities. It often involves the empowered developing confidence in their own capacities.

The term Human _________ covers a vast landscape of meanings, interpretations, definitions and disciplines ranging from psychology and philosophy to the highly commercialized Self-Help industry and Motivational sciences.

a. A Stake in the Outcome
b. AAAI
c. Empowerment
d. A4e

10. _________ means increasing the scope of a job through extending the range of its job duties and responsibilities. This contradicts the principles of specialisation and the division of labour whereby work is divided into small units, each of which is performed repetitively by an individual worker. Some motivational theories suggest that the boredom and alienation caused by the division of labour can actually cause efficiency to fall.
a. Centralization
b. Delayering
c. Mock interview
d. Job enlargement

11. _________ is an attempt to motivate employees by giving them the opportunity to use the range of their abilities. It is an idea that was developed by the American psychologist Frederick Herzberg in the 1950s. It can be contrasted to job enlargement which simply increases the number of tasks without changing the challenge.

a. Cash cow
b. C-A-K-E
c. Job enrichment
d. Catfish effect

12. _________ is, in very basic words, a position a firm occupies against its competitors.

According to Michael Porter, the three methods for creating a sustainable _________ are through:

1. Cost leadership

2. Differentiation

3. Focus (economics)

a. Competitive advantage
b. 28-hour day
c. 1990 Clean Air Act
d. Theory Z

13. In mathematical logic, _________ is a valid argument and rule of inference which makes the inference that, if the conjunction A and B is true, then A is true, and B is true.

In formal language:

$$A \wedge B \vdash A$$

or

$$A \wedge B \vdash B$$

The argument has one premise, namely a conjunction, and one often uses _________ in longer arguments to derive one of the conjuncts.

An example in English:

It's raining and it's pouring.

a. Validity
b. 1990 Clean Air Act
c. Fuzzy logic
d. Simplification

14. _________ describes the situation when output from (or information about the result of) an event or phenomenon in the past will influence the same event/phenomenon in the present or future. When an event is part of a chain of cause-and-effect that forms a circuit or loop, then the event is said to 'feed back' into itself.

_________ is also a synonym for:

- _________ signal; the information about the initial event that is the basis for subsequent modification of the event.
- _________ loop; the causal path that leads from the initial generation of the _________ signal to the subsequent modification of the event.

_________ is a mechanism, process or signal that is looped back to control a system within itself. Such a loop is called a _________ loop.

a. Positive feedback
b. 1990 Clean Air Act
c. Feedback loop
d. Feedback

15. _________ is one of the managerial functions like planning, organizing, staffing and directing. It is an important function because it helps to check the errors and to take the corrective action so that deviation from standards are minimized and stated goals of the organization are achieved in desired manner.According to modern concepts, _________ is a foreseeing action whereas earlier concept of _________ was used only when errors were detected. _________ in management means setting standards, measuring actual performance and taking corrective action.
a. Schedule of reinforcement
b. Turnover
c. Decision tree pruning
d. Control

16. _________ was developed by Frederick Herzberg, a psychologist who found that job satisfaction and job dissatisfaction acted independently of each other. _________ states that there are certain factors in the workplace that cause job satisfaction, while a separate set of factors cause dissatisfaction.

a. Need for Achievement
b. 1990 Clean Air Act
c. Two-factor theory
d. Need for power

17. A chief executive officer (_________) or chief executive is one of the highest-ranking corporate officer (executive) or administrator in charge of total management. An individual selected as President and _________ of a corporation, company, organization, or agency, reports to the board of directors. In internal communication and press releases, many companies capitalize the term and those of other high positions, even when they are not proper nouns.
a. Director of communications
b. Chief executive officer
c. CEO
d. Portfolio manager

18. In economics, _________ describes the state of a market with respect to competition.

- Perfect competition, in which the market consists of a very large number of firms producing a homogeneous product.
- Monopolistic competition where there are a large number of independent firms which have a very small proportion of the market share.
- Oligopoly, in which a market is dominated by a small number of firms which own more than 40% of the market share.
- Oligopsony, a market dominated by many sellers and a few buyers.
- Monopoly, where there is only one provider of a product or service.
- Natural monopoly, a monopoly in which economies of scale cause efficiency to increase continuously with the size of the firm. A firm is a natural monopoly if it is able to serve the entire market demand at a lower cost than any combination of two or more smaller, more specialized firms.
- Monopsony, when there is only one buyer in a market.

The imperfectly competitive structure is quite identical to the realistic market conditions where some monopolistic competitors, monopolists, oligopolists, and duopolists exist and dominate the market conditions. The elements of _________ include the number and size distribution of firms, entry conditions, and the extent of differentiation.

These somewhat abstract concerns tend to determine some but not all details of a specific concrete market system where buyers and sellers actually meet and commit to trade.

a. Productivity management
b. Deflation
c. Leading indicator
d. Market structure

19. _________, a business term, is a measure of how products and services supplied by a company meet or surpass customer expectation. It is seen as a key performance indicator within business and is part of the four perspectives of a Balanced Scorecard.

In a competitive marketplace where businesses compete for customers, _________ is seen as a key differentiator and increasingly has become a key element of business strategy.

a. Foreign ownership
b. Customer satisfaction
c. Horizontal integration
d. Critical Success Factor

20. A _________ is a working environment with conditions that are considered by many people of industrialized nations to be difficult or dangerous, usually where the workers have few opportunities to address their situation. This can include exposure to harmful materials, hazardous situations, extreme temperatures, or abuse from employers. _________ workers often work long hours for little pay, regardless of any laws mandating overtime pay or a minimum wage.

a. Continuous
b. Rate of return
c. Sweatshop
d. Complement

21. _________ is an approach whereby organizations make design-relevant decisions in a market and customer-oriented way as well as optimizing design-relevant (enterprise-)processes. It is a long-continuous comprehensive activity on all levels of business performance. _________ acts in the interface of management and design and functions as link between the platforms of technology, design, design thinking, management and marketing at internal and external interfaces of the enterprise.

a. Hierarchical organization
b. Fix it twice
c. Voice of the customer
d. Design Management

22. A _________ is a list of the general tasks and responsibilities of a position. Typically, it also includes to whom the position reports, specifications such as the qualifications needed by the person in the job, salary range for the position, etc. A _________ is usually developed by conducting a job analysis, which includes examining the tasks and sequences of tasks necessary to perform the job.

a. Recruitment
b. Recruitment Process Insourcing
c. Job description
d. Recruitment advertising

23. A _________ is a group of employees from various functional areas of the organization - research, engineering, marketing, finance. human resources, and operations, for example - who are all focused on a specific objective and are responsible to work as a team to improve coordination and innovation across divisions and resolve mutual problems.
a. Graduate recruitment
b. Sociotechnical systems
c. Cross-functional team
d. Goal-setting theory

24. _________ is a term originating in military organization theory, but now used more commonly in business management, particularly human resource management. _________ refers to the number of subordinates a supervisor has.

In the hierarchical business organization of the past it was not uncommon to see average spans of 1 to 10 or even less. That is, one manager supervised ten employees on average.

a. Span of control
b. Mentoring
c. CIFMS
d. Senior management

25. _________ is an idea in the field of Organizational studies and management which describes the psychology, attitudes, experiences, beliefs and Values (personal and cultural values) of an organization. It has been defined as 'the specific collection of values and norms that are shared by people and groups in an organization and that control the way they interact with each other and with stakeholders outside the organization.'

This definition continues to explain organizational values also known as 'beliefs and ideas about what kinds of goals members of an organization should pursue and ideas about the appropriate kinds or standards of behavior organizational members should use to achieve these goals. From organizational values develop organizational norms, guidelines or expectations that prescribe appropriate kinds of behavior by employees in particular situations and control the behavior of organizational members towards one another.'

_________ is not the same as corporate culture.

a. Organizational effectiveness
b. Union shop
c. Organizational development
d. Organizational culture

26. _________ is the process by which the activities of an organisation, particularly those regarding decision-making, become concentrated within a particular location and/or group.
a. Corner office
b. Product innovation
c. Chief operating officer
d. Centralization

27. In economics, business, retail, and accounting, a _________ is the value of money that has been used up to produce something, and hence is not available for use anymore. In economics, a _________ is an alternative that is given up as a result of a decision. In business, the _________ may be one of acquisition, in which case the amount of money expended to acquire it is counted as _________.
a. Cost allocation
b. Cost overrun
c. Fixed costs
d. Cost

28. _________ is the process of dispersing decision-making governance closer to the people or citizen. It includes the dispersal of administration or governance in sectors or areas like engineering, management science, political science, political economy, sociology and economics. _________ is also possible in the dispersal of population and employment.
a. Business plan
b. Formula for Change
c. Frenemy
d. Decentralization

29. In economics and especially in the theory of competition, _________ are obstacles in the path of a firm that make it difficult to enter a given market.

_________ are the source of a firm's pricing power - the ability of a firm to raise prices without losing all its customers.

The term refers to hindrances that an individual may face while trying to gain entrance into a profession or trade.

a. 1990 Clean Air Act
b. 28-hour day
c. Barriers to entry
d. Predatory pricing

30. _________ describes commerce transactions between businesses, such as between a manufacturer and a wholesaler, or between a wholesaler and a retailer. Contrasting terms are business-to-consumer (B2C) and business-to-government (B2G.)

The volume of B2B transactions is much higher than the volume of B2C transactions.

a. Category management
b. Market environment
c. Product bundling
d. Business-to-business

31. A _________ is a formal relationship between two or more parties to pursue a set of agreed upon goals or to meet a critical business need while remaining independent organizations.

Partners may provide the _________ with resources such as products, distribution channels, manufacturing capability, project funding, capital equipment, knowledge, expertise, or intellectual property. The alliance is a cooperation or collaboration which aims for a synergy where each partner hopes that the benefits from the alliance will be greater than those from individual efforts.

a. Farmshoring
b. Process automation
c. Golden parachute
d. Strategic alliance

32. _________ is subcontracting a process, such as product design or manufacturing, to a third-party company. The decision to outsource is often made in the interest of lowering cost or making better use of time and energy costs, redirecting or conserving energy directed at the competencies of a particular business, or to make more efficient use of land, labor, capital, (information) technology and resources. _________ became part of the business lexicon during the 1980s.

a. Unemployment insurance
b. Opinion leadership
c. Operant conditioning
d. Outsourcing

33. A _________ is a contemporary apporach to organizational design. It is an organization that is not defined by, or limited to, the horizontal, vertical, or external boundaries imposed by a predefined structure. This term was coined by former GE chairman Jack Welch because he wanted to eliminate vertical and horizontal boundaries within GE and break down external barriers between the company and its customers and suppliers.

a. Headquarters
b. Boundaryless organization
c. Business Roundtable
d. Chief risk officer

34. _________ refers to a (generally IT based) system for managing knowledge in organizations for supporting creation, capture, storage and dissemination of information. It can comprise a part (neither necessary or sufficient) of a Knowledge Management initiative.

The idea of a _________ is to enable employees to have ready access to the organization's documented base of facts, sources of information, and solutions.

a. 1990 Clean Air Act
b. 28-hour day
c. Knowledge management system
d. 33 Strategies of War

35. _________ is a business magazine published by McGraw-Hill. It was first published in 1929 (as The Business Week) under the direction of Malcolm Muir, who was serving as president of the McGraw-Hill Publishing company at the time. Its primary competitors in the national business magazine category are Fortune and Forbes, which are published bi-weekly.

a. BusinessWeek
b. The Wealth of Nations
c. Democracy in America
d. Hotel Vikas

36. _________ can be regarded as an outcome of mental processes (cognitive process) leading to the selection of a course of action among several alternatives. Every _________ process produces a final choice. The output can be an action or an opinion of choice.

a. 33 Strategies of War
b. 1990 Clean Air Act
c. 28-hour day
d. Decision making

37. _________ is the corporate management term for the act of reorganizing the legal, ownership, operational, or other structures of a company for the purpose of making it more profitable, or better organized for its present needs. Alternate reasons for _________ include a change of ownership or ownership structure, demerger repositioning debt _________ and financial _________.

a. Market value added
b. Net worth
c. Restructuring
d. Market value

38. _________ is a business management strategy, initially implemented by Motorola, that today enjoys widespread application in many sectors of industry.

_________ seeks to improve the quality of process outputs by identifying and removing the causes of defects (errors) and variation in manufacturing and business processes. It uses a set of quality management methods, including statistical methods, and creates a special infrastructure of people within the organization ('Black Belts' etc.)

a. Theory of constraints
b. Six Sigma
c. Takt time
d. Production line

1. _________ is one of the managerial functions like planning, organizing, staffing and directing. It is an important function because it helps to check the errors and to take the corrective action so that deviation from standards are minimized and stated goals of the organization are achieved in desired manner.According to modern concepts, _________ is a foreseeing action whereas earlier concept of _________ was used only when errors were detected. _________ in management means setting standards, measuring actual performance and taking corrective action.

a. Decision tree pruning
b. Schedule of reinforcement
c. Control
d. Turnover

2. _________ is, in very basic words, a position a firm occupies against its competitors.

According to Michael Porter, the three methods for creating a sustainable _________ are through:

1. Cost leadership

2. Differentiation

3. Focus (economics)

a. 28-hour day
b. Competitive advantage
c. 1990 Clean Air Act
d. Theory Z

3. _________ describes the situation when output from (or information about the result of) an event or phenomenon in the past will influence the same event/phenomenon in the present or future. When an event is part of a chain of cause-and-effect that forms a circuit or loop, then the event is said to 'feed back' into itself.

_________ is also a synonym for:

- _________ signal; the information about the initial event that is the basis for subsequent modification of the event.
- _________ loop; the causal path that leads from the initial generation of the _________ signal to the subsequent modification of the event.

_________ is a mechanism, process or signal that is looped back to control a system within itself. Such a loop is called a _________ loop.

a. Feedback loop
b. Feedback
c. 1990 Clean Air Act
d. Positive feedback

4. A chief executive officer (_________) or chief executive is one of the highest-ranking corporate officer (executive) or administrator in charge of total management. An individual selected as President and _________ of a corporation, company, organization, or agency, reports to the board of directors. In internal communication and press releases, many companies capitalize the term and those of other high positions, even when they are not proper nouns.

a. Chief executive officer
b. Director of communications
c. Portfolio manager
d. CEO

5. A _________ is a change implemented to address a weakness identified in a management system. Normally _________s are implemented in response to a customer complaint, abnormal levels of internal nonconformity, nonconformities identified during an internal audit or adverse or unstable trends in product and process monitoring such as would be identified by SPC.

The process of determining a _________ requires identification of actions that can be taken to prevent or mitigate the weakness.

a. 1990 Clean Air Act
b. 28-hour day
c. Zero defects
d. Corrective action

6. In business and accounting, _________s are everything of value that is owned by a person or company. Any property or object of value that one possesses, usually considered as applicable to the payment of one's debts is considered an _________. Simplistically stated, _________s are things of value that can be readily converted into cash.

a. A4e
b. A Stake in the Outcome
c. AAAI
d. Asset

7. The _________ is a financial ratio that measures whether or not a firm has enough resources to pay its debts over the next 12 months. It compares a firm's current assets to its current liabilities. It is expressed as follows:

$$\text{Current ratio} = \frac{\text{Current Assets}}{\text{Current Liabilities}}$$

For example, if WXY Company's current assets are $50,000,000 and its current liabilities are $40,000,000, then its _________ would be $50,000,000 divided by $40,000,000, which equals 1.25.

a. Current ratio
b. Financial ratio
c. Times interest earned
d. Return on assets

8. In accounting, _________ or sales profit is the difference between revenue and the cost of making a product or providing a service, before deducting overhead, payroll, taxation, and interest payments. Note that this is different from operating profit (earnings before interest and taxes.)

Net sales are calculated:

Net sales = Sales - Sales returns and allowances.

a. Gross profit margin
b. Cash flow
c. Capital budgeting
d. Gross profit

9. _________ is a financial ratio used to assess the profitability of a firm's core activities, excluding fixed costs.

The general calculation is:

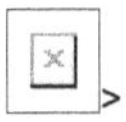

>

The _________ is related to the net profit margin, which assesses the profitability of an organization after including fixed costs.

_________ indicates the relationship between net sales revenue and the cost of goods sold.

a. Capital structure
b. Shareholder value
c. Sweat equity
d. Gross profit margin

10. In finance, _________ is borrowing money to supplement existing funds for investment in such a way that the potential positive or negative outcome is magnified and/or enhanced. It generally refers to using borrowed funds, or debt, so as to attempt to increase the returns to equity. Deleveraging is the action of reducing borrowings.
a. Limited liability corporation
b. Private equity
c. Limited partners
d. Gearing

11. Market _________ is a business, economics or investment term that refers to an asset's ability to be easily converted through an act of buying or selling without causing a significant movement in the price and with minimum loss of value. Money, or cash on hand, is the most liquid asset. An act of exchange of a less liquid asset with a more liquid asset is called liquidation.
a. 28-hour day
b. 33 Strategies of War
c. 1990 Clean Air Act
d. Liquidity

12. In finance, the _________ or quick ratio or liquid ratio measures the ability of a company to use its near cash or quick assets to immediately extinguish or retire its current liabilities. Quick assets include those current assets that presumably can be quickly converted to cash at close to their book values.

Generally, the acid test ratio should be 1:1 or better, however this varies widely by industry.

a. Acid-test
b. Inventory turnover
c. A4e
d. A Stake in the Outcome

13. _________, net margin, net _________ or net profit ratio all refer to a measure of profitability. It is calculated by finding the net profit as a percentage of the revenue.

$$\text{Net profit margin} = \frac{\text{Net profit (after taxes)}}{\text{Revenue}} \times 100\%$$

The _________ is mostly used for internal comparison.

a. Net profit margin
b. 1990 Clean Air Act
c. Profit maximization
d. Profit margin

14. _________ generally refers to a list of all planned expenses and revenues. It is a plan for saving and spending. A _________ is an important concept in microeconomics, which uses a _________ line to illustrate the trade-offs between two or more goods.

a. 28-hour day
b. 1990 Clean Air Act
c. 33 Strategies of War
d. Budget

15. In economics, business, retail, and accounting, a _________ is the value of money that has been used up to produce something, and hence is not available for use anymore. In economics, a _________ is an alternative that is given up as a result of a decision. In business, the _________ may be one of acquisition, in which case the amount of money expended to acquire it is counted as _________.

a. Fixed costs
b. Cost
c. Cost allocation
d. Cost overrun

16. An _________ is the annual budget of an activity stated in terms of Budget Classification Code, functional/subfunctional categories and cost accounts. It contains estimates of the total value of resources required for the performance of the operation including reimbursable work or services for others. It also includes estimates of workload in terms of total work units identified by cost accounts.

a. Inflation rate
b. Expected return
c. Operating budget
d. Expected gain

17. _________ has been described as the 'process of social influence in which one person can enlist the aid and support of others in the accomplishment of a common task' . A definition more inclusive of followers comes from Alan Keith of Genentech who said '_________ is ultimately about creating a way for people to contribute to making something extraordinary happen.'

_________ is one of the most salient aspects of the organizational context. However, defining _________ has been challenging.

a. Situational leadership
b. 28-hour day
c. Leadership
d. 1990 Clean Air Act

18. _________ is the process of dispersing decision-making governance closer to the people or citizen. It includes the dispersal of administration or governance in sectors or areas like engineering, management science, political science, political economy, sociology and economics. _________ is also possible in the dispersal of population and employment.

a. Frenemy
b. Decentralization
c. Formula for Change
d. Business plan

19. _________ is a process of agreeing upon objectives within an organization so that management and employees agree to the objectives and understand what they are in the organization.

The term '_________' was first popularized by Peter Drucker in his 1954 book 'The Practice of Management'.

The essence of _________ is participative goal setting, choosing course of actions and decision making.

a. Job enrichment
b. Management by objectives
c. Clean sheet review
d. Business economics

20. An _________ is a mostly hierarchical concept of subordination of entities that collaborate and contribute to serve one common aim.

Organizations are a variant of clustered entities. The structure of an organization is usually set up in many a styles, dependent on their objectives and ambience.

a. Informal organization
b. Organizational development
c. Open shop
d. Organizational structure

21. _________ is an advertisement in which a particular product specifically mentions a competitor by name for the express purpose of showing why the competitor is inferior to the product naming it.

This should not be confused with parody advertisements, where a fictional product is being advertised for the purpose of poking fun at the particular advertisement, nor should it be confused with the use of a coined brand name for the purpose of comparing the product without actually naming an actual competitor. ('Wikipedia tastes better and is less filling than the Encyclopedia Galactica.')

In the 1980s, during what has been referred to as the cola wars, soft-drink manufacturer Pepsi ran a series of advertisements where people, caught on hidden camera, in a blind taste test, chose Pepsi over rival Coca-Cola.

a. 33 Strategies of War
b. 1990 Clean Air Act
c. 28-hour day
d. Comparative advertising

22. _________, a business term, is a measure of how products and services supplied by a company meet or surpass customer expectation. It is seen as a key performance indicator within business and is part of the four perspectives of a Balanced Scorecard.

In a competitive marketplace where businesses compete for customers, _________ is seen as a key differentiator and increasingly has become a key element of business strategy.

a. Horizontal integration
b. Customer satisfaction
c. Critical Success Factor
d. Foreign ownership

23. _________ is an idea in the field of Organizational studies and management which describes the psychology, attitudes, experiences, beliefs and Values (personal and cultural values) of an organization. It has been defined as 'the specific collection of values and norms that are shared by people and groups in an organization and that control the way they interact with each other and with stakeholders outside the organization.'

This definition continues to explain organizational values also known as 'beliefs and ideas about what kinds of goals members of an organization should pursue and ideas about the appropriate kinds or standards of behavior organizational members should use to achieve these goals. From organizational values develop organizational norms, guidelines or expectations that prescribe appropriate kinds of behavior by employees in particular situations and control the behavior of organizational members towards one another.'

_________ is not the same as corporate culture.

a. Organizational effectiveness
b. Organizational culture
c. Union shop
d. Organizational development

24. A _________ is the term given to a company that facilitates the learning of its members and continuously transforms itself. _________s develop as a result of the pressures facing modern organizations and enables them to remain competitive in the business environment. A _________ has five main features; systems thinking, personal mastery, mental models, shared vision and team learning.

a. Learning organization
b. Quality function deployment
c. Hoshin Kanri
d. 1990 Clean Air Act

25. _________ is a process for determining and addressing needs, or gaps between current conditions and desired conditions organizations it is known as community needs analysis. It involves identifying material problems/deficits/weaknesses and advantages/opportunites/strengths, and evaluating possible solutions that take those qualities into consideration.

a. Needs assessment
b. 28-hour day
c. 1990 Clean Air Act
d. 33 Strategies of War

26. _________ is an area of knowledge within organizational theory that studies models and theories about the way an organization learns and adapts.

In Organizational development (OD), learning is a characteristic of an adaptive organization, i.e., an organization that is able to sense changes in signals from its environment (both internal and external) and adapt accordingly.

a. A4e
b. A Stake in the Outcome
c. AAAI
d. Organizational learning

27. In a military context, the _________ is the line of authority and responsibility along which orders are passed within a military unit and between different units. The term is also used in a civilian management context describing comparable hierarchical structures of authority.
a. Chain of command
b. 28-hour day
c. French leave
d. 1990 Clean Air Act

28. _________ is the process of comparing the cost, cycle time, productivity, or quality of a specific process or method to another that is widely considered to be an industry standard or best practice. Essentially, _________ provides a snapshot of the performance of your business and helps you understand where you are in relation to a particular standard. The result is often a business case for making changes in order to make improvements.
a. Benchmarking
b. Cost leadership
c. Competitive heterogeneity
d. Complementors

29. An _________ is a person who has possession of an enterprise and assumes significant accountability for the inherent risks and the outcome. It is an ambitious leader who combines land, labor, and capital to create and market new goods or services. The term is a loanword from French and was first defined by the Irish economist Richard Cantillon.
a. A4e
b. Entrepreneur
c. A Stake in the Outcome
d. AAAI

30. _________ according to Onuoha (2007) is the practice of starting new organizations or revitalizing mature organizations, particularly new businesses generally in response to identified opportunities. _________ is often a difficult undertaking, as a vast majority of new businesses fail. Entrepreneurial activities are substantially different depending on the type of organization that is being started.

a. Entrepreneurship
b. AAAI
c. A Stake in the Outcome
d. A4e

31. _________ is a business magazine published by McGraw-Hill. It was first published in 1929 (as The Business Week) under the direction of Malcolm Muir, who was serving as president of the McGraw-Hill Publishing company at the time. Its primary competitors in the national business magazine category are Fortune and Forbes, which are published bi-weekly.
a. The Wealth of Nations
b. Hotel Vikas
c. Democracy in America
d. BusinessWeek

32. _________ can be regarded as an outcome of mental processes (cognitive process) leading to the selection of a course of action among several alternatives. Every _________ process produces a final choice. The output can be an action or an opinion of choice.
a. 28-hour day
b. 1990 Clean Air Act
c. 33 Strategies of War
d. Decision making

33. _________ is the corporate management term for the act of reorganizing the legal, ownership, operational, or other structures of a company for the purpose of making it more profitable, or better organized for its present needs. Alternate reasons for _________ include a change of ownership or ownership structure, demerger repositioning debt _________ and financial _________.
a. Restructuring
b. Net worth
c. Market value added
d. Market value

1. _________ is an organization's process of defining its strategy and making decisions on allocating its resources to pursue this strategy, including its capital and people. Various business analysis techniques can be used in _________, including SWOT analysis (Strengths, Weaknesses, Opportunities, and Threats) and PEST analysis (Political, Economic, Social, and Technological analysis) or STEER analysis involving Socio-cultural, Technological, Economic, Ecological, and Regulatory factors and EPISTEL (Environment, Political, Informatic, Social, Technological, Economic and Legal)

_________ is the formal consideration of an organization's future course. All _________ deals with at least one of three key questions:

1. 'What do we do?'
2. 'For whom do we do it?'
3. 'How do we excel?'

In business _________, the third question is better phrased 'How can we beat or avoid competition?'. (Bradford and Duncan, page 1.)

a. 28-hour day
b. 1990 Clean Air Act
c. 33 Strategies of War
d. Strategic planning

2. In game theory, an _________ is a set of moves or strategies taken by the players, or their payoffs resulting from the actions or strategies taken by all players. The two are complementary in that given knowledge of the set of strategies of all players, the final state of the game is known, as are any relevant payoffs. In a game where chance or a random event is involved, the _________ is not known from only the set of strategies, but is only realized when the random event(s) are realized.

a. A4e
b. A Stake in the Outcome
c. AAAI
d. Outcome

3. The 'business case for _________', theorizes that in a global marketplace, a company that employs a diverse workforce (both men and women, people of many generations, people from ethnically and racially diverse backgrounds etc.) is better able to understand the demographics of the marketplace it serves and is thus better equipped to thrive in that marketplace than a company that has a more limited range of employee demographics.

An additional corollary suggests that a company that supports the _________ of its workforce can also improve employee satisfaction, productivity and retention.

a. Virtual team
b. Kanban
c. Trademark
d. Diversity

4. _________ is about the mental processes regarding choice, or choosing. It explains the processes that an individual undergoes to make choices. In organizational behavior study, _________ is a motivation theory first proposed by Victor Vroom of the Yale School of Management.
a. AAAI
b. Expectancy theory
c. A Stake in the Outcome
d. A4e

5. _________ is one of the managerial functions like planning, organizing, staffing and directing. It is an important function because it helps to check the errors and to take the corrective action so that deviation from standards are minimized and stated goals of the organization are achieved in desired manner.According to modern concepts, _________ is a foreseeing action whereas earlier concept of _________ was used only when errors were detected. _________ in management means setting standards, measuring actual performance and taking corrective action.
a. Schedule of reinforcement
b. Decision tree pruning
c. Turnover
d. Control

6. _________ was developed by Frederick Herzberg, a psychologist who found that job satisfaction and job dissatisfaction acted independently of each other. _________ states that there are certain factors in the workplace that cause job satisfaction, while a separate set of factors cause dissatisfaction.
a. Need for Achievement
b. 1990 Clean Air Act
c. Need for power
d. Two-factor theory

7. _________ can be regarded as an outcome of mental processes (cognitive process) leading to the selection of a course of action among several alternatives. Every _________ process produces a final choice. The output can be an action or an opinion of choice.

a. Decision making
b. 33 Strategies of War
c. 1990 Clean Air Act
d. 28-hour day

8. _________ is a term that has been used in various psychology theories, often in slightly different ways (e.g., Goldstein, Maslow, Rogers.) The term was originally introduced by the organismic theorist Kurt Goldstein for the motive to realise all of one's potentialities. In his view, it is the master motive--indeed, the only real motive a person has, all others being merely manifestations of it.
a. 33 Strategies of War
b. Self-actualization
c. 1990 Clean Air Act
d. 28-hour day

9. Maslow's _________ is a theory in psychology, proposed by Abraham Maslow in his 1943 paper A Theory of Human Motivation, which he subsequently extended to include his observations of humans' innate curiosity.

Maslow's _________ is predetermined in order of importance. It is often depicted as a pyramid consisting of five levels: the lowest level is associated with physiological needs, while the uppermost level is associated with self-actualization needs, particularly those related to identity and purpose. Deficiency needs must be met first. Once these are met, seeking to satisfy growth needs drives personal growth. The higher needs in this hierarchy only come into focus when the lower needs in the pyramid are met.

a. Hierarchy of needs
b. 1990 Clean Air Act
c. 33 Strategies of War
d. 28-hour day

10. _________ is an idea in the field of Organizational studies and management which describes the psychology, attitudes, experiences, beliefs and Values (personal and cultural values) of an organization. It has been defined as 'the specific collection of values and norms that are shared by people and groups in an organization and that control the way they interact with each other and with stakeholders outside the organization.'

This definition continues to explain organizational values also known as 'beliefs and ideas about what kinds of goals members of an organization should pursue and ideas about the appropriate kinds or standards of behavior organizational members should use to achieve these goals. From organizational values develop organizational norms, guidelines or expectations that prescribe appropriate kinds of behavior by employees in particular situations and control the behavior of organizational members towards one another.'

_________ is not the same as corporate culture.

a. Organizational development
b. Organizational effectiveness
c. Union shop
d. Organizational culture

11. In law, _________ is the term to describe a partnership between two or more parties.

In England a number of statutes on the subject have been passed, the chief being the Bastardy Act of 1845, and the Bastardy Laws Amendment Acts of 1872 and 1873. The mother of a bastard may summon the putative father to petty sessions within twelve months of the birth (or at any later time if he is proved to have contributed to the child's support within twelve months after the birth), and the justices, as after hearing evidence on both sides, may, if the mother's evidence be corroborated in some material particular, adjudge the man to be the putative father of the child, and order him to pay a sum not exceeding five shillings a week for its maintenance, together with a sum for expenses incidental to the birth, or the funeral expenses, if it has died before the date of order, and the costs of the proceedings.

a. Affirmative action
b. Affiliation
c. Abraham Harold Maslow
d. Adam Smith

12. _________ refers to an individual's desire for significant accomplishment, mastering of skills, control, or high standards. The term was introduced by the psychologist, David McClelland.

_________ is related to the difficulty of tasks people choose to undertake.

a. Need for power
b. Two-factor theory
c. 1990 Clean Air Act
d. Need for achievement

13. _________ attempts to explain relational satisfaction in terms of perceptions of fair/unfair distributions of resources within interpersonal relationships. _________ is considered as one of the justice theories, It was first developed in 1962 by John Stacey Adams, a workplace and behavioral psychologist, who asserted that employees seek to maintain equity between the inputs that they bring to a job and the outcomes that they receive from it against the perceived inputs and outcomes of others (Adams, 1965.) The belief is that people value fair treatment which causes them to be motivated to keep the fairness maintained within the relationships of their co-workers and the organization.

a. A4e
b. AAAI
c. A Stake in the Outcome
d. Equity theory

14. _________ has become one of the most popular theories in organizational psychology.

Goal setting has been a formula used for acheivement since the early 1800s. The form and pattern has cahanged drastically over the years and there is still much debate as to what is the most efective pattern to follow.

a. Job satisfaction
b. Human relations
c. Corporate Culture
d. Goal-setting theory

15. _________ describes the situation when output from (or information about the result of) an event or phenomenon in the past will influence the same event/phenomenon in the present or future. When an event is part of a chain of cause-and-effect that forms a circuit or loop, then the event is said to 'feed back' into itself.

_________ is also a synonym for:

- _________ signal; the information about the initial event that is the basis for subsequent modification of the event.
- _________ loop; the causal path that leads from the initial generation of the _________ signal to the subsequent modification of the event.

_________ is a mechanism, process or signal that is looped back to control a system within itself. Such a loop is called a _________ loop.

a. Positive feedback
b. Feedback
c. Feedback loop
d. 1990 Clean Air Act

16. _________ is the use of consequences to modify the occurrence and form of behavior. _________ is distinguished from classical conditioning (also called respondent conditioning, or Pavlovian conditioning) in that _________ deals with the modification of 'voluntary behavior' or operant behavior. Operant behavior 'operates' on the environment and is maintained by its consequences, while classical conditioning deals with the conditioning of respondent behaviors which are elicited by antecedent conditions.

a. Outsourcing
b. Occupational Safety and Health Administration
c. Unemployment insurance
d. Operant conditioning

17. In operant conditioning, _________ occurs when an event following a response causes an increase in the probability of that response occurring in the future. Response strength can be assessed by measures such as the frequency with which the response is made (for example, a pigeon may peck a key more times in the session), or the speed with which it is made (for example, a rat may run a maze faster.) The environment change contingent upon the response is called a reinforcer.

a. Historiometry
b. Diminishing Manufacturing Sources and Material Shortages
c. Meetings, Incentives, Conferences, and Exhibitions
d. Reinforcement

18. _________ refers to training in different ways to improve overall performance. It takes advantage of the particular effectiveness of each training method, while at the same time attempting to neglect the shortcomings of that method by combining it with other methods that address its weaknesses.

Cross training is employee-employer field means, training employees to do one another's work.

a. 28-hour day
b. 1990 Clean Air Act
c. 33 Strategies of War
d. Cross-training

19. _________ is learning that occurs as a function of observing, retaining and, in the case of imitation learning, replicating novel behavior executed by others. It is most associated with the work of psychologist Albert Bandura, who implemented some of the seminal studies in the area and initiated social learning theory. It involves the process of learning to copy or model the action of another through observing another doing it.

a. AAAI
b. A Stake in the Outcome
c. Observational learning
d. A4e

20. _________ is the belief that one is capable of performing in a certain manner to attain certain goals. It is a belief that one has the capabilities to execute the courses of actions required to manage prospective situations. Unlike efficacy, which is the power to produce an effect (in essence, competence), _________ is the belief (whether or not accurate) that one has the power to produce that effect.

a. 1990 Clean Air Act
b. 33 Strategies of War
c. 28-hour day
d. Self-efficacy

21. In psychology, _________ reflects a person's overall evaluation or appraisal of his or her own worth.

_________ encompasses beliefs (for example, 'I am competent/incompetent') and emotions (for example, triumph/despair, pride/shame.) Behavior may reflect _________

a. 33 Strategies of War
b. 1990 Clean Air Act
c. 28-hour day
d. Self-esteem

22. _________, sometimes referred to as 'cumulative causation', is a feedback loop system in which the system responds to perturbation in the same direction as the perturbation. In contrast, a system that responds to the perturbation in the opposite direction is called a negative feedback system. These concepts were first recognized as broadly applicable by Norbert Wiener in his 1948 work on cybernetics.

a. Feedback loop
b. 1990 Clean Air Act
c. Negative feedback
d. Positive feedback

23. _________ is the theory that people learn new behavior through overt reinforcement or punishment, or via observational learning of the social actors in their environment. If people observe positive, desired outcomes in the observed behavior, they are more likely to model, imitate, and adopt the behavior themselves.

_________ is derived from the work of Gabriel Tarde (1843-1904) which proposed that social learning occurred through four main stages of limitation:

- close contact,
- imitation of superiors,
- understanding of concepts,
- role model behaviour

It consists of 3 parts observing, imitating, and reinforcements

Julian Rotter moved away from theories based on psychosis and behaviourism, and developed a learning theory. In Social Learning and Clinical Psychology (1954), Rotter suggests that the effect of behaviour has an impact on the motivation of people to engage in that specific behaviour.

a. 28-hour day
b. 33 Strategies of War
c. 1990 Clean Air Act
d. Social learning theory

24. _________ is a term describing performance-related pay, most frequently in the context of educational reform. It provides bonuses for workers who perform their jobs better, according to measurable criteria. In the United States, policy makers are divided on whether _________ should be offered to public school teachers, as is commonly the case in the United Kingdom.

a. Real wage
b. Performance-related pay
c. Profit-sharing agreement
d. Merit pay

25. An _________ is a mostly hierarchical concept of subordination of entities that collaborate and contribute to serve one common aim.

Organizations are a variant of clustered entities. The structure of an organization is usually set up in many a styles, dependent on their objectives and ambience.

a. Informal organization
b. Open shop
c. Organizational development
d. Organizational structure

26. A _________ is a form of periodic payment from an employer to an employee, which may be specified in an employment contract. It is contrasted with piece wages, where each job, hour or other unit is paid separately, rather than on a periodic basis.

From the point of a view of running a business, _________ can also be viewed as the cost of acquiring human resources for running operations, and is then termed personnel expense or _________ expense.

a. Salary
b. Human resource management
c. Human resources
d. Training and development

27. An _________ is a call option on the common stock of a company, issued as a form of non-cash compensation. Restrictions on the option (such as vesting and limited transferability) attempt to align the holder's interest with those of the business' shareholders. If the company's stock rises, holders of options experience a direct financial benefit.
a. AAAI
b. A4e
c. Employee stock option
d. A Stake in the Outcome

28. In finance, an _________ is a contract between a buyer and a seller that gives the buyer the right--but not the obligation--to buy or to sell a particular asset (the underlying asset) at a later day at an agreed price. In return for granting the _________, the seller collects a payment (the premium) from the buyer. A call _________ gives the buyer the right to buy the underlying asset; a put _________ gives the buyer of the _________ the right to sell the underlying asset.
a. AAAI
b. A4e
c. A Stake in the Outcome
d. Option

29. In a military context, the _________ is the line of authority and responsibility along which orders are passed within a military unit and between different units. The term is also used in a civilian management context describing comparable hierarchical structures of authority.
a. French leave
b. 1990 Clean Air Act
c. 28-hour day
d. Chain of command

30. _________ is a business magazine published by McGraw-Hill. It was first published in 1929 (as The Business Week) under the direction of Malcolm Muir, who was serving as president of the McGraw-Hill Publishing company at the time. Its primary competitors in the national business magazine category are Fortune and Forbes, which are published bi-weekly.

a. The Wealth of Nations
b. Democracy in America
c. Hotel Vikas
d. BusinessWeek

31. _________ has been described as the 'process of social influence in which one person can enlist the aid and support of others in the accomplishment of a common task' . A definition more inclusive of followers comes from Alan Keith of Genentech who said '_________ is ultimately about creating a way for people to contribute to making something extraordinary happen.'

_________ is one of the most salient aspects of the organizational context. However, defining _________ has been challenging.

a. Situational leadership
b. Leadership
c. 1990 Clean Air Act
d. 28-hour day

1. _________ has been described as the 'process of social influence in which one person can enlist the aid and support of others in the accomplishment of a common task' . A definition more inclusive of followers comes from Alan Keith of Genentech who said '_________ is ultimately about creating a way for people to contribute to making something extraordinary happen.'

_________ is one of the most salient aspects of the organizational context. However, defining _________ has been challenging.

a. 1990 Clean Air Act
b. Situational leadership
c. Leadership
d. 28-hour day

2. _________ is a forward looking process for setting goals and regularly checking progress toward achieving those goals. It is a continual feedback process whereby the actual outputs are measured and compared with the desired goals. Any discrepancy or gap is then fed back into changing the inputs of the process, so as to achieve the desired goals or outputs.

a. 33 Strategies of War
b. Performance management
c. 1990 Clean Air Act
d. 28-hour day

3. _________ is a term used to describe any moral, political that stresses human interdependence and the importance of a collective, rather than the importance of separate individuals. Collectivists focus on community and society, and seek to give priority to group goals over individual goals. The philosophical underpinnings of _________ are for some related to holism or organicism - the view that the whole is greater than the sum of its parts/pieces.

a. 28-hour day
b. 1990 Clean Air Act
c. Collaborative methods
d. Collectivism

4. _________ is an idea in the field of Organizational studies and management which describes the psychology, attitudes, experiences, beliefs and Values (personal and cultural values) of an organization. It has been defined as 'the specific collection of values and norms that are shared by people and groups in an organization and that control the way they interact with each other and with stakeholders outside the organization.'

This definition continues to explain organizational values also known as 'beliefs and ideas about what kinds of goals members of an organization should pursue and ideas about the appropriate kinds or standards of behavior organizational members should use to achieve these goals. From organizational values develop organizational norms, guidelines or expectations that prescribe appropriate kinds of behavior by employees in particular situations and control the behavior of organizational members towards one another.'

_________ is not the same as corporate culture.

a. Organizational development
b. Organizational effectiveness
c. Organizational culture
d. Union shop

5. _________ is one of the managerial functions like planning, organizing, staffing and directing. It is an important function because it helps to check the errors and to take the corrective action so that deviation from standards are minimized and stated goals of the organization are achieved in desired manner.According to modern concepts, _________ is a foreseeing action whereas earlier concept of _________ was used only when errors were detected. _________ in management means setting standards, measuring actual performance and taking corrective action.

a. Decision tree pruning
b. Turnover
c. Schedule of reinforcement
d. Control

6. _________ refers to increasing the spiritual, political, social or economic strength of individuals and communities. It often involves the empowered developing confidence in their own capacities.

The term Human _________ covers a vast landscape of meanings, interpretations, definitions and disciplines ranging from psychology and philosophy to the highly commercialized Self-Help industry and Motivational sciences.

a. A Stake in the Outcome
b. A4e
c. AAAI
d. Empowerment

7. _________ is individual power based on a high level of identification with, admiration of, or respect for the powerholder.

Nationalism, Patriotism, Celebrities and well-respected people are examples of _________ in effect.

_________ is one of the Five Bases of Social Power, as defined by Bertram Raven and his colleagues[1] in 1959.

a. 28-hour day
b. Referent power
c. 1990 Clean Air Act
d. 33 Strategies of War

8. _________ is, in very basic words, a position a firm occupies against its competitors.

According to Michael Porter, the three methods for creating a sustainable _________ are through:

1. Cost leadership

2. Differentiation

3. Focus (economics)

a. 1990 Clean Air Act
b. 28-hour day
c. Theory Z
d. Competitive advantage

9. _________ of the learning curve effect and the closely related experience curve effect express the relationship between equations for experience and efficiency or between efficiency gains and investment in the effort. The experience of 'learning curves' was first observed by the 19th Century German psychologist Hermann Ebbinghaus according to the difficulty of memorizing varying numbers of verbal stimuli, and subsequent learning about the complex processes of learning are discussed in the

.

The rule used for representing the learning curve effect states that the more times a task has been performed, the less time will be required on each subsequent iteration.

a. Models
b. Point biserial correlation coefficient
c. Distribution
d. Spatial Decision Support Systems

10. The _________ is a leadership theory in the field of organizational studies developed by Robert House in 1971 and revised in 1996. The theory that a leader's behavior is contingent to the satisfaction, motivation and performance of subordinates. The revised version also argues that the leader engage in behaviors that complement subordinate's abilities and compensate for deficiencies.

a. Path-goal theory
b. Human relations
c. Corporate Culture
d. Sociotechnical systems

11. _________ is a leadership style that defines as leadership that creates voluble and positive change in the followers. A transformational leader focuses on 'transforming' others to help each other, to look out for each other, be encouraging, harmonious, and look out for the organization as a whole. In this leadership, the leader enhances the motivation, moral and performance of his follower group.

a. Strong-Campbell Interest Inventory
b. SESAMO
c. Polynomial conjoint measurement
d. Transformational leadership

12. The 'business case for _________', theorizes that in a global marketplace, a company that employs a diverse workforce (both men and women, people of many generations, people from ethnically and racially diverse backgrounds etc.) is better able to understand the demographics of the marketplace it serves and is thus better equipped to thrive in that marketplace than a company that has a more limited range of employee demographics.

An additional corollary suggests that a company that supports the _________ of its workforce can also improve employee satisfaction, productivity and retention.

a. Kanban
b. Virtual team
c. Trademark
d. Diversity

13. _________ is a term used to classify a group leadership theories that inquire the interactions between leaders and followers. A transactional leader focuses more on a series of 'transactions'. This person is interested in looking out for oneself, having exchange benefits with their subordinates and clarify a sense of duty with rewards and punishments to reach goals.

a. 33 Strategies of War
b. Transactional leadership
c. 28-hour day
d. 1990 Clean Air Act

14. _________ , often measured as an _________ Quotient (EQ), is a term that describes the ability, capacity, skill or (in the case of the trait _________ model) a self-perceived ability, to identify, assess, and manage the emotions of one's self, of others, and of groups. Different models have been proposed for the definition of _________ and disagreement exists as to how the term should be used. Despite these disagreements, which are often highly technical, the ability _________ and trait _________ models (but not the mixed models) are enjoying considerable support in the literature and have successful applications in many different domains.
a. A Stake in the Outcome
b. AAAI
c. Emotional intelligence
d. A4e

15. _________ is a business magazine published by McGraw-Hill. It was first published in 1929 (as The Business Week) under the direction of Malcolm Muir, who was serving as president of the McGraw-Hill Publishing company at the time. Its primary competitors in the national business magazine category are Fortune and Forbes, which are published bi-weekly.
a. BusinessWeek
b. Democracy in America
c. The Wealth of Nations
d. Hotel Vikas

16. _________ can be regarded as an outcome of mental processes (cognitive process) leading to the selection of a course of action among several alternatives. Every _________ process produces a final choice. The output can be an action or an opinion of choice.
a. 33 Strategies of War
b. 28-hour day
c. Decision making
d. 1990 Clean Air Act

1. _________ is the concept of how effective an organization is in achieving the outcomes the organization intends to produce. The idea of _________ is especially important for non-profit organizations as most people who donate money to non-profit organizations and charities are interested in knowing whether the organization is effective in accomplishing its goals.

An organization's effectiveness is also dependent on its communicative competence and ethics.

a. Informal organization
b. Organizational development
c. Organizational effectiveness
d. Organizational structure

2. _________ is, in very basic words, a position a firm occupies against its competitors.

According to Michael Porter, the three methods for creating a sustainable _________ are through:

1. Cost leadership

2. Differentiation

3. Focus (economics)

a. 1990 Clean Air Act
b. Theory Z
c. 28-hour day
d. Competitive advantage

3. _________ is the term used to describe a situation where different entities cooperate advantageously for a final outcome. Simply defined, it means that the whole is greater than the sum of the individual parts. Although the whole will be greater than each individual part, this is not the concept of _________.
a. 33 Strategies of War
b. 28-hour day
c. 1990 Clean Air Act
d. Synergy

4. _________ is one of the managerial functions like planning, organizing, staffing and directing. It is an important function because it helps to check the errors and to take the corrective action so that deviation from standards are minimized and stated goals of the organization are achieved in desired manner.According to modern concepts, _________ is a foreseeing action whereas earlier concept of _________ was used only when errors were detected. _________ in management means setting standards, measuring actual performance and taking corrective action.

a. Control
b. Schedule of reinforcement
c. Turnover
d. Decision tree pruning

5. A _________ is a group of employees from various functional areas of the organization - research, engineering, marketing, finance. human resources, and operations, for example - who are all focused on a specific objective and are responsible to work as a team to improve coordination and innovation across divisions and resolve mutual problems.
a. Goal-setting theory
b. Graduate recruitment
c. Sociotechnical systems
d. Cross-functional team

6. In mathematics, a _________ law is (roughly speaking) a formal power series behaving as if it were the product of a Lie group. They were first defined in 1946 by S. Bochner. The term _________ sometimes means the same as _________ law, and sometimes means one of several generalizations.
a. 28-hour day
b. 1990 Clean Air Act
c. 33 Strategies of War
d. Formal group

7. _________ is a type of thought exhibited by group members who try to minimize conflict and reach consensus without critically testing, analyzing, and evaluating ideas. Individual creativity, uniqueness, and independent thinking are lost in the pursuit of group cohesiveness, as are the advantages of reasonable balance in choice and thought that might normally be obtained by making decisions as a group. During _________, members of the group avoid promoting viewpoints outside the comfort zone of consensus thinking.
a. Psychological statistics
b. Self-report inventory
c. Groupthink
d. Diffusion of responsibility

8. _________ is an idea in the field of Organizational studies and management which describes the psychology, attitudes, experiences, beliefs and Values (personal and cultural values) of an organization. It has been defined as 'the specific collection of values and norms that are shared by people and groups in an organization and that control the way they interact with each other and with stakeholders outside the organization.'

This definition continues to explain organizational values also known as 'beliefs and ideas about what kinds of goals members of an organization should pursue and ideas about the appropriate kinds or standards of behavior organizational members should use to achieve these goals. From organizational values develop organizational norms, guidelines or expectations that prescribe appropriate kinds of behavior by employees in particular situations and control the behavior of organizational members towards one another.'

_________ is not the same as corporate culture.

a. Organizational development
b. Union shop
c. Organizational effectiveness
d. Organizational culture

9. A _________ -- also known as a geographically dispersed team -- is a group of individuals who work across time, space, and organizational boundaries with links strengthened by webs of communication technology. They have complementary skills and are committed to a common purpose, have interdependent performance goals, and share an approach to work for which they hold themselves mutually accountable. Geographically dispersed teams allow organizations to hire and retain the best people regardless of location.

a. Kanban
b. Risk management
c. Trademark
d. Virtual team

10. _________ is the study of groups, and also a general term for group processes. Relevant to the fields of psychology, sociology, and communication studies, a group is two or more individuals who are connected to each other by social relationships. Because they interact and influence each other, groups develop a number of dynamic processes that separate them from a random collection of individuals.

a. 1990 Clean Air Act
b. Collective action
c. 28-hour day
d. Group dynamics

11. _________ is an increasingly broadening term with which an organization, or other human system describes the combination of traditionally administrative personnel functions with acquisition and application of skills, knowledge and experience, Employee Relations and resource planning at various levels. The field draws upon concepts developed in Industrial/Organizational Psychology and System Theory. _________ has at least two related interpretations depending on context. The original usage derives from political economy and economics, where it was traditionally called labor, one of four factors of production although this perspective is changing as a function of new and ongoing research into more strategic approaches at national levels. This first usage is used more in terms of '_________ development', and can go beyond just organizations to the level of nations . The more traditional usage within corporations and businesses refers to the individuals within a firm or agency, and to the portion of the organization that deals with hiring, firing, training, and other personnel issues, typically referred to as `_________ management'.

a. Human resource management
b. Progressive discipline
c. Bradford Factor
d. Human resources

12. The 'business case for _________', theorizes that in a global marketplace, a company that employs a diverse workforce (both men and women, people of many generations, people from ethnically and racially diverse backgrounds etc.) is better able to understand the demographics of the marketplace it serves and is thus better equipped to thrive in that marketplace than a company that has a more limited range of employee demographics.

An additional corollary suggests that a company that supports the _________ of its workforce can also improve employee satisfaction, productivity and retention.

a. Trademark
b. Diversity
c. Virtual team
d. Kanban

13. In economics and sociology, an _________ is any factor (financial or non-financial) that enables or motivates a particular course of action, or counts as a reason for preferring one choice to the alternatives. It is an expectation that encourages people to behave in a certain way. Since human beings are purposeful creatures, the study of _________ structures is central to the study of all economic activity (both in terms of individual decision-making and in terms of co-operation and competition within a larger institutional structure.)

a. AAAI
b. A4e
c. Incentive
d. A Stake in the Outcome

14. _________ is a forward looking process for setting goals and regularly checking progress toward achieving those goals. It is a continual feedback process whereby the actual outputs are measured and compared with the desired goals. Any discrepancy or gap is then fed back into changing the inputs of the process, so as to achieve the desired goals or outputs.

a. 28-hour day
b. 1990 Clean Air Act
c. Performance management
d. 33 Strategies of War

15. In the social psychology of groups, _________ is the phenomenon of people making less effort to achieve a goal when they work in a group than when they work alone. This is seen as one of the main reasons groups are sometimes less productive than the combined performance of their members working as individuals.

- Ringelmann, Max : 1913

Research began in 1913 with Max Ringelmann's study. He found that when he asked a group of men to pull on a rope, that they did not pull as hard, or put as much effort into the activity, as they did when they were pulling alone.

a. Social loafing
b. Machiavellianism
c. Personal space
d. Self-enhancement

16. _________ is a business magazine published by McGraw-Hill. It was first published in 1929 (as The Business Week) under the direction of Malcolm Muir, who was serving as president of the McGraw-Hill Publishing company at the time. Its primary competitors in the national business magazine category are Fortune and Forbes, which are published bi-weekly.

a. Democracy in America
b. Hotel Vikas
c. The Wealth of Nations
d. BusinessWeek

17. _________ can be regarded as an outcome of mental processes (cognitive process) leading to the selection of a course of action among several alternatives. Every _________ process produces a final choice. The output can be an action or an opinion of choice.

a. 28-hour day
b. 1990 Clean Air Act
c. 33 Strategies of War
d. Decision making

1. _________ is an increasingly broadening term with which an organization, or other human system describes the combination of traditionally administrative personnel functions with acquisition and application of skills, knowledge and experience, Employee Relations and resource planning at various levels. The field draws upon concepts developed in Industrial/Organizational Psychology and System Theory. _________ has at least two related interpretations depending on context. The original usage derives from political economy and economics, where it was traditionally called labor, one of four factors of production although this perspective is changing as a function of new and ongoing research into more strategic approaches at national levels. This first usage is used more in terms of '_________ development', and can go beyond just organizations to the level of nations . The more traditional usage within corporations and businesses refers to the individuals within a firm or agency, and to the portion of the organization that deals with hiring, firing, training, and other personnel issues, typically referred to as `_________ management'.

a. Progressive discipline
b. Human resource management
c. Human resources
d. Bradford Factor

2. _________ is a forward looking process for setting goals and regularly checking progress toward achieving those goals. It is a continual feedback process whereby the actual outputs are measured and compared with the desired goals. Any discrepancy or gap is then fed back into changing the inputs of the process, so as to achieve the desired goals or outputs.

a. 28-hour day
b. Performance management
c. 33 Strategies of War
d. 1990 Clean Air Act

3. The field of _________ looks at the relationship between management and workers, particularly groups of workers represented by a union.

_________ is an important factor in analyzing 'varieties of capitalism', such as neocorporatism, social democracy, and neoliberalism

a. Informal organization
b. Industrial relations
c. Organizational effectiveness
d. Overtime

4. _________ is a method by which the job performance of an employee is evaluated _________ is a part of career development.

_________s are regular reviews of employee performance within organizations

Generally, the aims of a _________ are to:

- Give feedback on performance to employees.
- Identify employee training needs.
- Document criteria used to allocate organizational rewards.
- Form a basis for personnel decisions: salary increases, promotions, disciplinary actions, etc.
- Provide the opportunity for organizational diagnosis and development.
- Facilitate communication between employee and administraton
- Validate selection techniques and human resource policies to meet federal Equal Employment Opportunity requirements.

A common approach to assessing performance is to use a numerical or scalar rating system whereby managers are asked to score an individual against a number of objectives/attributes. In some companies, employees receive assessments from their manager, peers, subordinates and customers while also performing a self assessment.

a. Human resource management
b. Personnel management
c. Progressive discipline
d. Performance appraisal

5. _________ refers to the process of screening, and selecting qualified people for a job at an organization or firm mid- and large-size organizations and companies often retain professional recruiters or outsource some of the process to _________ agencies. External _________ is the process of attracting and selecting employees from outside the organization.

The _________ industry has four main types of agencies: employment agencies, _________ websites and job search engines, 'headhunters' for executive and professional _________, and in-house _________.

a. Referral recruitment
b. Recruitment Process Outsourcing
c. Labour hire
d. Recruitment

6. _________ is a business management strategy, initially implemented by Motorola, that today enjoys widespread application in many sectors of industry.

_________ seeks to improve the quality of process outputs by identifying and removing the causes of defects (errors) and variation in manufacturing and business processes. It uses a set of quality management methods, including statistical methods, and creates a special infrastructure of people within the organization ('Black Belts' etc.)

a. Theory of constraints
b. Takt time
c. Production line
d. Six Sigma

7. _________ is one of the managerial functions like planning, organizing, staffing and directing. It is an important function because it helps to check the errors and to take the corrective action so that deviation from standards are minimized and stated goals of the organization are achieved in desired manner.According to modern concepts, _________ is a foreseeing action whereas earlier concept of _________ was used only when errors were detected. _________ in management means setting standards, measuring actual performance and taking corrective action.

a. Schedule of reinforcement
b. Control
c. Decision tree pruning
d. Turnover

8. _________ describes the situation when output from (or information about the result of) an event or phenomenon in the past will influence the same event/phenomenon in the present or future. When an event is part of a chain of cause-and-effect that forms a circuit or loop, then the event is said to 'feed back' into itself.

_________ is also a synonym for:

- _________ signal; the information about the initial event that is the basis for subsequent modification of the event.
- _________ loop; the causal path that leads from the initial generation of the _________ signal to the subsequent modification of the event.

_________ is a mechanism, process or signal that is looped back to control a system within itself. Such a loop is called a _________ loop.

a. Positive feedback
b. Feedback loop
c. Feedback
d. 1990 Clean Air Act

9. _________ is the strategic and coherent approach to the management of an organisation's most valued assets - the people working there who individually and collectively contribute to the achievement of the objectives of the business. The terms '_________' and 'human resources' (HR) have largely replaced the term 'personnel management' as a description of the processes involved in managing people in organizations. In simple sense, _________ means employing people, developing their resources, utilizing, maintaining and compensating their services in tune with the job and organizational requirement.

a. Progressive discipline
b. Job knowledge
c. Revolving door syndrome
d. Human resource management

10. An _________ is a mostly hierarchical concept of subordination of entities that collaborate and contribute to serve one common aim.

Organizations are a variant of clustered entities. The structure of an organization is usually set up in many a styles, dependent on their objectives and ambience.

a. Organizational structure
b. Informal organization
c. Open shop
d. Organizational development

11. The 'business case for _________', theorizes that in a global marketplace, a company that employs a diverse workforce (both men and women, people of many generations, people from ethnically and racially diverse backgrounds etc.) is better able to understand the demographics of the marketplace it serves and is thus better equipped to thrive in that marketplace than a company that has a more limited range of employee demographics.

An additional corollary suggests that a company that supports the _________ of its workforce can also improve employee satisfaction, productivity and retention.

a. Diversity
b. Kanban
c. Virtual team
d. Trademark

12. There are two types of _________ relationships: formal and informal. Informal relationships develop on their own between partners. Formal _________, on the other hand, refers to assigned relationships, often associated with organizational _________ programs designed to promote employee development or to assist at-risk children and youth.

a. Mentoring
b. Real Property Administrator
c. Fix it twice
d. Human resource management system

13. The _________ of 1967, Pub. L. No. 90-202, 81 Stat. 602 (Dec. 15, 1967), codified as Chapter 14 of Title 29 of the United States Code, 29 U.S.C. Â§ 621 through 29 U.S.C. Â§ 634 (ADEA), prohibits employment discrimination against persons 40 years of age or older in the United States). The law also sets standards for pensions and benefits provided by employers and requires that information about the needs of older workers be provided to the general public.

a. Undue hardship
b. Extra time
c. Unemployment and Farm Relief Act
d. Age Discrimination in Employment Act

14. _________ is a contract between two parties, one being the employer and the other being the employee. An employee may be defined as: 'A person in the service of another under any contract of hire, express or implied, oral or written, where the employer has the power or right to control and direct the employee in the material details of how the work is to be performed.' Black's Law Dictionary page 471 (5th ed. 1979.)

a. Exit interview
b. Employment counsellor
c. Employment rate
d. Employment

15. The _________ 1970 is an Act of the United Kingdom Parliament which prohibits any less favourable treatment between men and women in terms of pay and conditions of employment. It came into force on 29 December 1975. The term pay is interpreted in a broad sense to include, on top of wages, things like holidays, pension rights, company perks and some kinds of bonuses.

a. Equal Pay Act
b. Oncale v. Sundowner Offshore Services
c. Architectural Barriers Act of 1968
d. Australian labour law

16. _________ occurs when expectant women are fired, not hired, or otherwise discriminated against due to their pregnancy or intention to become pregnant. Common forms of _________ include not being hired due to visible pregnancy or likelihood of becoming pregnant, being fired after informing an employer of one's pregnancy, being fired after maternity leave, and receiving a pay dock due to pregnancy. In the United States, since 1978, employers are legally bound to provide what insurance, leave pay, and additional support that would be bestowed upon any employee with medical leave or disability.

a. 33 Strategies of War
b. 1990 Clean Air Act
c. 28-hour day
d. Pregnancy Discrimination

17. In economics, _________ is the desire to own something and the ability to pay for it. The term _________ signifies the ability or the willingness to buy a particular commodity at a given point of time.

a. 28-hour day
b. 33 Strategies of War
c. 1990 Clean Air Act
d. Demand

18. _________ is the activity of estimating the quantity of a product or service that consumers will purchase. _________ involves techniques including both informal methods, such as educated guesses, and quantitative methods, such as the use of historical sales data or current data from test markets. _________ may be used in making pricing decisions, in assessing future capacity requirements, or in making decisions on whether to enter a new market.

a. 28-hour day
b. Demand forecasting
c. Profitability index
d. 1990 Clean Air Act

19. _________ is the process of estimation in unknown situations. Prediction is a similar, but more general term. Both can refer to estimation of time series, cross-sectional or longitudinal data.

a. 28-hour day
b. 1990 Clean Air Act
c. 33 Strategies of War
d. Forecasting

20. _________ refers to various methodologies for analyzing the requirements of a job.

The general purpose of _________ is to document the requirements of a job and the work performed. Job and task analysis is performed as a basis for later improvements, including: definition of a job domain; describing a job; developing performance appraisals, selection systems, promotion criteria, training needs assessment, and compensation plans.

a. Management process
b. Work design
c. Hersey-Blanchard situational theory
d. Job analysis

21. _________ is subcontracting a process, such as product design or manufacturing, to a third-party company. The decision to outsource is often made in the interest of lowering cost or making better use of time and energy costs, redirecting or conserving energy directed at the competencies of a particular business, or to make more efficient use of land, labor, capital, (information) technology and resources. _________ became part of the business lexicon during the 1980s.

a. Operant conditioning
b. Unemployment insurance
c. Opinion leadership
d. Outsourcing

22. A _________ is a list of the general tasks and responsibilities of a position. Typically, it also includes to whom the position reports, specifications such as the qualifications needed by the person in the job, salary range for the position, etc. A _________ is usually developed by conducting a job analysis, which includes examining the tasks and sequences of tasks necessary to perform the job.

a. Job description
b. Recruitment Process Insourcing
c. Recruitment
d. Recruitment advertising

23. A chief executive officer (_________) or chief executive is one of the highest-ranking corporate officer (executive) or administrator in charge of total management. An individual selected as President and _________ of a corporation, company, organization, or agency, reports to the board of directors. In internal communication and press releases, many companies capitalize the term and those of other high positions, even when they are not proper nouns.

a. CEO
b. Portfolio manager
c. Chief executive officer
d. Director of communications

24. A _________ is a quantitative research method commonly employed in survey research. The aim of this approach is to ensure that each interviewee is presented with exactly the same questions in the same order. This ensures that answers can be reliably aggregated and that comparisons can be made with confidence between sample subgroups or between different survey periods.

a. Questionnaire construction
b. Structured interview
c. Questionnaire
d. Mystery shoppers

25. _________ are a method of interviews where questions can be changed or adapted to meet the respondent's intelligence, understanding or belief. Unlike a structured interview they do not offer a limited, pre-set range of answers for a respondent to choose, but instead advocate listening to how each individual person responds to the question.

The method to gather information using this technique is fairly limited, for example most surveys that are carried out via telephone or even in person tend to follow a structured method.

a. Unstructured interviews
b. A Stake in the Outcome
c. A4e
d. AAAI

26. The term _________ in logic applies to arguments or statements.

An argument is valid if and only if the truth of its premises entails the truth of its conclusion, it would be self-contradictory to affirm the premises and deny the conclusion. The corresponding conditional of a valid argument is a logical truth and the negation of its corresponding conditional is a contradiction.

a. Validity
b. Fuzzy logic
c. 1990 Clean Air Act
d. Simplification

27. _________ is a system of training a new generation of practitioners of a skill. Apprentices (or in early modern usage 'prentices') or prot>ég>és build their careers from _________s. Most of their training is done on the job while working for an employer who helps the apprentices learn their trade, in exchange for their continuing labour for an agreed period after they become skilled.
a. Apprenticeship
b. A Stake in the Outcome
c. AAAI
d. A4e

28. _________ is a process for determining and addressing needs, or gaps between current conditions and desired conditions organizations it is known as community needs analysis. It involves identifying material problems/deficits/weaknesses and advantages/opportunites/strengths, and evaluating possible solutions that take those qualities into consideration.

a. 1990 Clean Air Act
b. 33 Strategies of War
c. Needs assessment
d. 28-hour day

29. _________ can be regarded as an outcome of mental processes (cognitive process) leading to the selection of a course of action among several alternatives. Every _________ process produces a final choice. The output can be an action or an opinion of choice.
a. 33 Strategies of War
b. 28-hour day
c. 1990 Clean Air Act
d. Decision making

30. A _________ is a compensation, usually financial, received by a worker in exchange for their labor.

Compensation in terms of _________s is given to worker and compensation in terms of salary is given to employees. Compensation is a monetary benefits given to employees in returns of the services provided by them.

a. Profit-sharing agreement
b. State Compensation Insurance Fund
c. Performance-related pay
d. Wage

31. A _________ or chief executive is one of the highest-ranking corporate officer (executive) or administrator in charge of total management. An individual selected as President and _________ of a corporation, company, organization, or agency, reports to the board of directors. In internal communication and press releases, many companies capitalize the term and those of other high positions, even when they are not proper nouns.
a. Purchasing manager
b. Financial analyst
c. Chief executive officer
d. Chief brand officer

32. While _________ literally refers to a person responsible for the performance of duties involved in running an organization, the exact meaning of the role is variable, depending on the organization.

While there is no clear line between executive or principal and inferior officers, principal officers are high-level officials in the executive branch of U.S. government such as department heads of independent agencies. In Humphrey's Executor v. United States, 295 U.S. 602 (1935), the Court distinguished between _________s and quasi-legislative or quasi-judicial officers by stating that the former serve at the pleasure of the President and may be removed at his discretion.

a. Easement
b. Australian Fair Pay and Conditions Standard
c. Unreported employment
d. Executive officer

33. _________ and Theory Y are theories of human motivation created and developed by Douglas McGregor at the MIT Sloan School of Management in the 1960s that have been used in human resource management, organizational behavior, organizational communication and organizational development. They describe two very different attitudes toward workforce motivation. McGregor felt that companies followed either one or the other approach.

In _________, which many managers practice, management assumes employees are inherently lazy and will avoid work if they can. They inherently dislike work. Because of this, workers need to be closely supervised and comprehensive systems of controls developed.

a. Theory X
b. Job enrichment
c. Management team
d. Cash cow

34. _________ occurs when a person is available to work and seeking work but currently without work. The prevalence of _________ is usually measured using the _________ rate, which is defined as the percentage of those in the labor force who are unemployed. The _________ rate is also used in economic studies and economic indexes such as the United States' Conference Board's Index of Leading Indicators as a measure of the state of the macroeconomics.

a. Outplacement
b. Employment-to-population ratio
c. Unemployment Convention, 1919
d. Unemployment

35. _________ are payments made by governments or other authorized bodies to unemployed people. It may be based on a compulsory para-governmental insurance system. Depending on the jurisdiction and the status of the person, those sums may be meager, covering only basic needs (thus a form of basic welfare), or may compensate the lost pay somewhat proportionally to the previous earned salary.

a. Outplacement
b. Unemployment compensation
c. Unemployment insurance
d. Unemployment benefits

36. In organized labor, _________ is the method whereby workers organize together (usually in unions) to meet, converse, and negotiate upon the work conditions with their employers normally resulting in a written contract setting forth the wages, hours, and other conditions to be observed for a stipulated period.It is the practice in which union and company representatives meet to negotiate a new labor contract. In various national labor and employment law contexts, the term _________ takes on a more specific legal meaning. In a broad sense, however, it is the coming together of workers to negotiate their employment.
a. Labor rights
b. Paid time off
c. Collective bargaining
d. Labour law

37. _________ is a business magazine published by McGraw-Hill. It was first published in 1929 (as The Business Week) under the direction of Malcolm Muir, who was serving as president of the McGraw-Hill Publishing company at the time. Its primary competitors in the national business magazine category are Fortune and Forbes, which are published bi-weekly.
a. Democracy in America
b. Hotel Vikas
c. The Wealth of Nations
d. BusinessWeek

1. A _________ is a subset of the overall internal controls of a business covering the application of people, documents, technologies, and procedures by management accountants to solving business problems such as costing a product, service or a business-wide strategy. _________s are distinct from regular information systems in that they are used to analyze other information systems applied in operational activities in the organization. Academically, the term is commonly used to refer to the group of information management methods tied to the automation or support of human decision making, e.g. Decision Support Systems, Expert systems, and Executive information systems.

a. 1990 Clean Air Act
b. Strategic information system
c. 28-hour day
d. Management information system

2. _________ is one of the managerial functions like planning, organizing, staffing and directing. It is an important function because it helps to check the errors and to take the corrective action so that deviation from standards are minimized and stated goals of the organization are achieved in desired manner.According to modern concepts, _________ is a foreseeing action whereas earlier concept of _________ was used only when errors were detected. _________ in management means setting standards, measuring actual performance and taking corrective action.

a. Control
b. Schedule of reinforcement
c. Decision tree pruning
d. Turnover

3. _________ can be regarded as an outcome of mental processes (cognitive process) leading to the selection of a course of action among several alternatives. Every _________ process produces a final choice. The output can be an action or an opinion of choice.

a. 33 Strategies of War
b. 28-hour day
c. Decision making
d. 1990 Clean Air Act

4. _________ is an idea in the field of Organizational studies and management which describes the psychology, attitudes, experiences, beliefs and Values (personal and cultural values) of an organization. It has been defined as 'the specific collection of values and norms that are shared by people and groups in an organization and that control the way they interact with each other and with stakeholders outside the organization.'

This definition continues to explain organizational values also known as 'beliefs and ideas about what kinds of goals members of an organization should pursue and ideas about the appropriate kinds or standards of behavior organizational members should use to achieve these goals. From organizational values develop organizational norms, guidelines or expectations that prescribe appropriate kinds of behavior by employees in particular situations and control the behavior of organizational members towards one another.'

_________ is not the same as corporate culture.

a. Union shop
b. Organizational effectiveness
c. Organizational development
d. Organizational culture

5. _________ is, in very basic words, a position a firm occupies against its competitors.

According to Michael Porter, the three methods for creating a sustainable _________ are through:

1. Cost leadership

2. Differentiation

3. Focus (economics)

a. Theory Z
b. Competitive advantage
c. 1990 Clean Air Act
d. 28-hour day

6. _________ describes the situation when output from (or information about the result of) an event or phenomenon in the past will influence the same event/phenomenon in the present or future. When an event is part of a chain of cause-and-effect that forms a circuit or loop, then the event is said to 'feed back' into itself.

_________ is also a synonym for:

- _________ signal; the information about the initial event that is the basis for subsequent modification of the event.
- _________ loop; the causal path that leads from the initial generation of the _________ signal to the subsequent modification of the event.

_________ is a mechanism, process or signal that is looped back to control a system within itself. Such a loop is called a _________ loop.

a. 1990 Clean Air Act
b. Feedback loop
c. Feedback
d. Positive feedback

7. _________ is a recursive process where two or more people or organizations work together in an intersection of common goals -- for example, an intellectual endeavor that is creative in nature--by sharing knowledge, learning and building consensus. _________ does not require leadership and can sometimes bring better results through decentralization and egalitarianism. In particular, teams that work collaboratively can obtain greater resources, recognition and reward when facing competition for finite resources._________ is also present in opposing goals exhibiting the notion of adversarial _________, though this is not a common case for using the term.

a. Collectivism
b. 1990 Clean Air Act
c. 28-hour day
d. Collaboration

8. _________, e-commuting, e-work, telework, working from home (WFH), or working at home (WAH) is a work arrangement in which employees enjoy flexibility in working location and hours. In other words, the daily commute to a central place of work is replaced by telecommunication links. Many work from home, while others, occasionally also referred to as nomad workers or web commuters utilize mobile telecommunications technology to work from coffee shops or myriad other locations.

a. 1990 Clean Air Act
b. 28-hour day
c. Telecommuting
d. 33 Strategies of War

9. In economics, business, retail, and accounting, a _________ is the value of money that has been used up to produce something, and hence is not available for use anymore. In economics, a _________ is an alternative that is given up as a result of a decision. In business, the _________ may be one of acquisition, in which case the amount of money expended to acquire it is counted as _________.

a. Fixed costs
b. Cost allocation
c. Cost overrun
d. Cost

10. _________ is the intelligence of machines and the branch of computer science which aims to create it. Major _________ textbooks define the field as 'the study and design of intelligent agents,' where an intelligent agent is a system that perceives its environment and takes actions which maximize its chances of success. John McCarthy, who coined the term in 1956, defines it as 'the science and engineering of making intelligent machines.'

The field was founded on the claim that a central property of human beings, intelligence--the sapience of Homo sapiens--can be so precisely described that it can be simulated by a machine.

a. A4e
b. AAAI
c. A Stake in the Outcome
d. Artificial intelligence

11. An _________ is a mostly hierarchical concept of subordination of entities that collaborate and contribute to serve one common aim.

Organizations are a variant of clustered entities. The structure of an organization is usually set up in many a styles, dependent on their objectives and ambience.

a. Organizational structure
b. Open shop
c. Informal organization
d. Organizational development

12. _________ constitute a class of computer-based information systems including knowledge-based systems that support decision-making activities.

_________ are a specific class of computerized information systems that supports business and organizational decision-making activities. A properly-designed _________ is an interactive software-based system intended to help decision makers compile useful information from raw data, documents, personal knowledge, and/or business models to identify and solve problems and make decisions.

a. 1990 Clean Air Act
b. 28-hour day
c. Decision support systems
d. Spatial Decision Support Systems

13. An _________ is software that attempts to reproduce the performance of one or more human experts, most commonly in a specific problem domain, and is a traditional application and/or subfield of artificial intelligence. A wide variety of methods can be used to simulate the performance of the expert however common to most or all are 1) the creation of a so-called 'knowledgebase' which uses some knowledge representation formalism to capture the Subject Matter Experts (SME) knowledge and 2) a process of gathering that knowledge from the SME and codifying it according to the formalism, which is called knowledge engineering. _________s may or may not have learning components but a third common element is that once the system is developed it is proven by being placed in the same real world problem solving situation as the human SME, typically as an aid to human workers or a supplement to some information system.

a. Expert system
b. A Stake in the Outcome
c. A4e
d. AAAI

14. _________ is an increasingly broadening term with which an organization, or other human system describes the combination of traditionally administrative personnel functions with acquisition and application of skills, knowledge and experience, Employee Relations and resource planning at various levels. The field draws upon concepts developed in Industrial/Organizational Psychology and System Theory. _________ has at least two related interpretations depending on context. The original usage derives from political economy and economics, where it was traditionally called labor, one of four factors of production although this perspective is changing as a function of new and ongoing research into more strategic approaches at national levels. This first usage is used more in terms of '_________ development', and can go beyond just organizations to the level of nations . The more traditional usage within corporations and businesses refers to the individuals within a firm or agency, and to the portion of the organization that deals with hiring, firing, training, and other personnel issues, typically referred to as `_________ management'.
a. Human resource management
b. Progressive discipline
c. Bradford Factor
d. Human resources

15. _________ refers to various methodologies for analyzing the requirements of a job.

The general purpose of _________ is to document the requirements of a job and the work performed. Job and task analysis is performed as a basis for later improvements, including: definition of a job domain; describing a job; developing performance appraisals, selection systems, promotion criteria, training needs assessment, and compensation plans.

a. Work design
b. Job analysis
c. Management process
d. Hersey-Blanchard situational theory

1. _________ is an area of business concerned with the production of goods and services, and involves the responsibility of ensuring that business operations are efficient in terms of using as little resource as needed, and effective in terms of meeting customer requirements. It is concerned with managing the process that converts inputs (in the forms of materials, labour and energy) into outputs (in the form of goods and services.)

Operations traditionally refers to the production of goods and services separately, although the distinction between these two main types of operations is increasingly difficult to make as manufacturers tend to merge product and service offerings.

a. Operations management
b. A Stake in the Outcome
c. AAAI
d. A4e

2. _________ is, in very basic words, a position a firm occupies against its competitors.

According to Michael Porter, the three methods for creating a sustainable _________ are through:

1. Cost leadership

2. Differentiation

3. Focus (economics)

a. Theory Z
b. 28-hour day
c. 1990 Clean Air Act
d. Competitive advantage

3. A _________ is a computer program typically used to provide some form of artificial intelligence, which consists primarily of a set of rules about behavior. These rules, termed productions, are a basic representation found useful in AI planning, expert systems and action selection. A _________ provides the mechanism necessary to execute productions in order to achieve some goal for the system.

a. Production system
b. 1990 Clean Air Act
c. 33 Strategies of War
d. 28-hour day

4. _________ is one of the managerial functions like planning, organizing, staffing and directing. It is an important function because it helps to check the errors and to take the corrective action so that deviation from standards are minimized and stated goals of the organization are achieved in desired manner.According to modern concepts, _________ is a foreseeing action whereas earlier concept of _________ was used only when errors were detected. _________ in management means setting standards, measuring actual performance and taking corrective action.

a. Decision tree pruning
b. Control
c. Turnover
d. Schedule of reinforcement

5. _________, a business term, is a measure of how products and services supplied by a company meet or surpass customer expectation. It is seen as a key performance indicator within business and is part of the four perspectives of a Balanced Scorecard.

In a competitive marketplace where businesses compete for customers, _________ is seen as a key differentiator and increasingly has become a key element of business strategy.

a. Horizontal integration
b. Foreign ownership
c. Critical Success Factor
d. Customer satisfaction

6. _________ consists of the processes a company uses to track and organize its contacts with its current and prospective customers. _________ software is used to support these processes; information about customers and customer interactions can be entered, stored and accessed by employees in different company departments. Typical _________ goals are to improve services provided to customers, and to use customer contact information for targeted marketing.

a. Marketing plan
b. Green marketing
c. Customer relationship management
d. Disruptive technology

7. Quality management can be considered to have three main components: quality control, quality assurance and _________. Quality management is focused not only on product quality, but also the means to achieve it. Quality management therefore uses quality assurance and control of processes as well as products to achieve more consistent quality.

a. Quality management
b. 1990 Clean Air Act
c. Quality improvement
d. 28-hour day

8. _________ refers to metrics and measures of output from production processes, per unit of input. Labor _________, for example, is typically measured as a ratio of output per labor-hour, an input. _________ may be conceived of as a metrics of the technical or engineering efficiency of production.
a. Productivity
b. Value engineering
c. Master production schedule
d. Remanufacturing

9. In economics, _________ (TFP) is a variable which accounts for effects in total output not caused by inputs. For example, a year with unusually good weather will tend to have higher output, because bad weather hinders agricultural output. A variable like weather does not directly relate to unit inputs, so weather is considered a _________ variable.
a. Total-factor productivity
b. Collaborative Planning, Forecasting and Replenishment
c. Strict liability
d. Minimax

10. A _________ system is a manufacturing system in which there is some amount of flexibility that allows the system to react in the case of changes, whether predicted or unpredicted. This flexibility is generally considered to fall into two categories, which both contain numerous subcategories.

The first category, machine flexibility, covers the system's ability to be changed to produce new product types, and ability to change the order of operations executed on a part. The second category is called routing flexibility, which consists of the ability to use multiple machines to perform the same operation on a part, as well as the system's ability to absorb large-scale changes, such as in volume, capacity, or capability.

a. Flexible manufacturing
b. Jidoka
c. Manufacturing resource planning
d. Homeworkers

11. _________ is the amount of goods and services that a labourer produces in a given amount of time. It is one of several types of productivity that economists measure. _________ can be measured for a firm, a process or a country.

a. Retroactive overtime
b. Time and attendance
c. Labour productivity
d. Business Network Transformation

12. In economics, business, retail, and accounting, a _________ is the value of money that has been used up to produce something, and hence is not available for use anymore. In economics, a _________ is an alternative that is given up as a result of a decision. In business, the _________ may be one of acquisition, in which case the amount of money expended to acquire it is counted as _________.
a. Fixed costs
b. Cost overrun
c. Cost
d. Cost allocation

13. _________ is a concept related to lean and just-in-time (JIT) production. The Japanese word _________ is a common term meaning 'signboard' or 'billboard'. According to Taiichi Ohno, the man credited with developing JIT, _________ is a means through which JIT is achieved.
a. Risk management
b. Trademark
c. Kanban
d. Succession planning

14. _________ is an inventory strategy that strives to improve the return on investment of a business by reducing in-process inventory and its associated carrying costs. To meet _________ objectives, the process relies on signals between different points in the process. This means the process is often driven by a series of signals, or Kanban , which tell production when to make the next part. Kanban are usually 'tickets' but can be simple visual signals, such as the presence or absence of a part on a shelf. Implemented correctly, _________ can dramatically improve a manufacturing organization's return on investment, quality, and efficiency.
a. 1990 Clean Air Act
b. 28-hour day
c. Just-in-time
d. 33 Strategies of War

15. _________ is an idea in the field of Organizational studies and management which describes the psychology, attitudes, experiences, beliefs and Values (personal and cultural values) of an organization. It has been defined as 'the specific collection of values and norms that are shared by people and groups in an organization and that control the way they interact with each other and with stakeholders outside the organization.'

This definition continues to explain organizational values also known as 'beliefs and ideas about what kinds of goals members of an organization should pursue and ideas about the appropriate kinds or standards of behavior organizational members should use to achieve these goals. From organizational values develop organizational norms, guidelines or expectations that prescribe appropriate kinds of behavior by employees in particular situations and control the behavior of organizational members towards one another.'

_________ is not the same as corporate culture.

a. Organizational development
b. Organizational effectiveness
c. Organizational culture
d. Union shop

16. _________ is a business magazine published by McGraw-Hill. It was first published in 1929 (as The Business Week) under the direction of Malcolm Muir, who was serving as president of the McGraw-Hill Publishing company at the time. Its primary competitors in the national business magazine category are Fortune and Forbes, which are published bi-weekly.
a. BusinessWeek
b. Democracy in America
c. Hotel Vikas
d. The Wealth of Nations

17. A _________ is a set of companies with interlocking business relationships and shareholdings. It is a type of business group.

The prototypical _________ are those which appeared in Japan during the 'economic miracle' following World War II.

a. 33 Strategies of War
b. 28-hour day
c. 1990 Clean Air Act
d. Keiretsu

18. _________ can be regarded as an outcome of mental processes (cognitive process) leading to the selection of a course of action among several alternatives. Every _________ process produces a final choice. The output can be an action or an opinion of choice.

a. 28-hour day
b. 33 Strategies of War
c. 1990 Clean Air Act
d. Decision making

Chapter 1

1. b	2. b	3. a	4. c	5. d	6. d	7. a	8. a	9. b	10. d
11. d	12. d	13. c	14. d	15. d	16. d	17. d	18. d	19. d	20. d
21. d	22. d	23. a	24. c	25. b	26. c	27. d	28. c	29. d	30. a
31. b	32. d	33. d	34. d	35. d	36. a	37. d	38. b	39. a	

Chapter 2

1. d	2. d	3. d	4. b	5. b	6. d	7. d	8. a	9. d	10. d
11. d	12. d	13. a	14. d	15. d	16. a	17. b	18. d	19. d	20. d
21. b	22. d	23. d	24. d	25. d	26. d				

Chapter 3

1. c	2. b	3. b	4. b	5. d	6. c	7. d	8. d	9. d	10. d
11. d	12. c	13. b	14. b	15. c	16. d	17. d	18. c	19. a	20. b
21. b	22. d	23. b	24. d	25. d	26. d	27. d			

Chapter 4

1. b	2. c	3. d	4. b	5. c	6. d	7. c	8. d	9. d	10. c
11. d	12. d	13. b	14. d	15. d	16. d	17. d	18. d	19. d	20. c
21. d	22. a	23. c	24. d	25. c	26. d	27. c	28. c	29. d	30. b
31. d									

Chapter 5

1. b	2. b	3. c	4. d	5. c	6. c	7. a	8. b	9. c	10. d
11. d	12. b	13. c	14. c	15. c	16. d	17. d	18. d	19. d	20. d
21. c	22. d	23. d	24. d	25. c					

Chapter 6

1. d	2. a	3. a	4. a	5. d	6. b	7. d	8. d	9. d	10. c
11. d	12. b	13. d	14. d	15. c	16. d	17. d	18. d	19. d	20. a
21. b	22. b	23. a	24. b	25. c	26. d	27. d	28. b	29. b	

Chapter 7

1. d	2. d	3. b	4. c	5. d	6. a	7. d	8. d	9. c	10. d
11. c	12. a	13. d	14. d	15. d	16. c	17. c	18. d	19. b	20. c
21. d	22. c	23. c	24. a	25. d	26. d	27. d	28. d	29. c	30. d
31. d	32. d	33. b	34. c	35. a	36. d	37. c	38. b		

Chapter 8

1. c	2. b	3. b	4. d	5. d	6. d	7. a	8. d	9. d	10. d
11. d	12. a	13. d	14. d	15. b	16. c	17. c	18. b	19. b	20. d
21. d	22. b	23. b	24. a	25. a	26. d	27. a	28. a	29. b	30. a
31. d	32. d	33. a							

Chapter 9

1. d	2. d	3. d	4. b	5. d	6. d	7. a	8. b	9. a	10. d
11. b	12. d	13. d	14. d	15. b	16. d	17. d	18. d	19. c	20. d
21. d	22. d	23. d	24. d	25. d	26. a	27. c	28. d	29. d	30. d
31. b									

Chapter 10

1. c	2. b	3. d	4. c	5. d	6. d	7. b	8. d	9. a	10. a
11. d	12. d	13. b	14. c	15. a	16. c				

Chapter 11

1. c	2. d	3. d	4. a	5. d	6. d	7. c	8. d	9. d	10. d
11. d	12. b	13. c	14. c	15. a	16. d	17. d			

Chapter 12

1. c	2. b	3. b	4. d	5. d	6. d	7. b	8. c	9. d	10. a
11. a	12. a	13. d	14. d	15. a	16. d	17. d	18. b	19. d	20. d
21. d	22. a	23. a	24. b	25. a	26. a	27. a	28. c	29. d	30. d
31. c	32. d	33. a	34. d	35. d	36. c	37. d			

Chapter 13

1. d	2. a	3. c	4. d	5. b	6. c	7. d	8. c	9. d	10. d
11. a	12. c	13. a	14. d	15. b					

Chapter 14

1. a	2. d	3. a	4. b	5. d	6. c	7. c	8. a	9. a	10. a
11. c	12. c	13. c	14. c	15. c	16. a	17. d	18. d		

www.ingramcontent.com/pod-product-compliance
Lightning Source LLC
Chambersburg PA
CBHW082048230426
43670CB00016B/2815